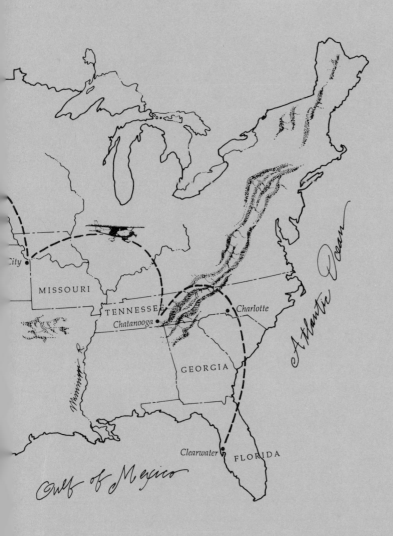

WHEELS UP!

Adventures of a Private Pilot

James D. Nisbet

Other Books by James D. Nisbet

High Temperature Alloy Exploratory Research
The Entrepreneur
The Dow is Dead
Weathering Stock Market Storms
Boyhood on a Farm

Published by
New River Press
645 Fairmount Street
Woonsocket, R.I.02895
(800) 244-1257

Library of Congress
Catalog Card Number:

ISBN 1-891724-00-2

Cover Photo by Wally Prelle

IN MEMORY OF MY FLYING COMPANIONS

ACKNOWLEDGMENTS

Many thanks to Carol Hazard for editing the first manuscript, to Bruce Bowers, a retired TWA pilot, for his technical editing and to Linda Winecoff for drawing the maps. Thanks to my son Jack who called me a year ago with an invitation I couldn't turn down. Jack said, "Join me in Atlanta next week where I will be renting a 2-ton truck and picking up my furniture and moving it to Spokane. We can trade-off the driving and finally edit your new book by reading it to each other and correcting it during the six day junket." I said, "Jack it's a deal." It is not often in this busy age that an eighty year old father and a forty eight year old son can find the time for such companionship.

4

Contents

PREFACE

People who live in a golden age usually complain how yellow everything looks.

That, at least, was the opinion of the late North Carolina poet and teacher Randall Jarrell. Prof. Jarrell, however, never knew our author, his fellow Carolinian James D. Nisbet.

In *Wheels Up*, Mr. Nisbet puts his arm around our shoulders, scoops us into his small plane and pilots us through the golden age of American aviation from the inside. But everything looks far more than yellow! It's bright, alive, thrilling and intimately personal. We become part of his family. We hurtle with him "through the soup" and feel the pride every time he "greases it on." We share the successes and the failures, the smiles and the tears.

To be frank, before I read it, I couldn't imagine liking this book.

For one thing, despite Mr. Nisbet's distinguished career in science and industry, it's the memoir of a relatively ordinary person. Curmudgeonly, middle-aged editors like me don't like – let alone publish — the memoirs of relatively ordinary people. Yet, every time I read it, I find that *Wheels Up* carries me along with the power of its anecdotes, its wry wit, its sometimes hair-raising aerial escapades, its occasional tragedies and its all-around warmth.

It's a memoir for people who don't like memoirs.

Many of us, especially middle-aged editors, tend to look down upon life with a cynical, if-only-they-knew smile. Mr. Nisbet looks down upon life, too, but from one of the most positive possible perspectives: joyfully from an airplane.

Paul F. Eno
Woonsocket, Rhode Island
December 1997

Paul F. Eno, formerly of The Providence Journal-Bulletin, *is an author, editor and publisher.*

1

DREAMING ABOUT FLYING

A World War I Ace

It was a warm July day in 1923 when I caught the flying bug. I was six years old and my brother Oliver was seven, and we were playing in the sandbox in the backyard of our house in Van Wyck, South Carolina. That old sandbox wasn't like the one my grandchildren have today, with so many toys you can't see the sand. We had very few toys: a pail, a shovel and a mold for making little bricks.

We were building a beehive-shaped kiln like the one Mr. Ashe had at his brickyard down the road. When we couldn't get the right mixture of water and sand to hold the bricks together, Huss Barber slipped us a bucket of cement. Huss was building a brick foundation for a new corn crib down beside the barn. He told us to mix a bucket of cement with five buckets of sand and wet it just a little.

"Don't let it go liquid!" Huss warned. After we'd made 100 good, firm bricks and set them aside to dry, our dad came out and told us he had to go to Charlotte to buy some parts for the tractor.

Then he astounded us.

"Maybe you boys would like to come along. On the way home we could stop and see Col. Elliot Springs fly under the new Buster Boyd Bridge!"

I was on my feet like a shot. "Hurry up, Oliver, let's go. I want to see an airplane!"

I held out my arms as though flying as my dirty bare feet padded toward the house. All the excitement woke Lion, our German Shepherd, who was sleeping in the shade of a black walnut tree, out of the hot July sun. Barking, Lion jumped up and ran with us toward the house.

Mother intercepted us at the door.

"Before you can come in the house you must wash your hands and feet, then put on your shoes and clean overalls."

That just took a jiffy. Then we bounded out to the side yard, arms held straight out, hopped up on the running board and jumped into the back seat of the car.

Dad came out and cranked the Model-T Ford by hand. Fortunately, the car wasn't "cranky" that day and it started right away. He stepped on the running board and then into the car.

We were off!

We couldn't travel faster than 35 miles per hour on those dirt roads because we had to avoid the ruts, but we didn't have to worry about potholes.

Following the World War I armistice in 1918, Col. Elliot Springs had stayed in Europe for a year, carousing in Paris, before returning home to settle down with his parents and work for his father in Fort Mill, S.C., his hometown.

The colonel's father, Leroy Springs, was a well known textile manufacturer who had cotton mills in several towns in that part of the Carolinas.

When the celebrated World War I ace came home from Paris, he continued to get a lot of publicity. He bought his own airplane and flew it from a private landing strip in a field next to his father's house.

When a new bridge opened on the recently paved highway #29 over the Catawba River, between Charlotte and Gastonia, North Carolina, it was named after a prominent politician: The Buster Boyd Bridge. Local newspaper reporters dared Col. Springs to fly under the bridge to celebrate its opening, and the flamboyant ace agreed to try it. The time was set for high noon on the day we took off for Charlotte.

Dad had read aloud to us all the newspaper publicity that preceded the flight, and we had begged to go see it, but Dad said he was too busy running the farm. When he came up with that excuse to go to Charlotte for tractor parts, we knew he wanted to see the stunt as much as we did.

After Dad finished shopping, we headed out Route #29 for the Catawba River to see the show. Traffic was heavy. As we traveled slowly along, we saw numerous cars pulled off the road with flat tires. Back in those days, it was hard to drive very far without a flat. When we got within a mile of the river, traffic came to a standstill.

Dad parked the car on the shoulder of the road and we walked the rest of the way.

There were throngs of people gathering on both sides of the river. Governors Cameron Morrison of North Carolina and Thomas McLeod of South Carolina were present, along with the majors of surrounding Carolina towns.

The people waited for the scheduled high-noon flight, but noon came and went with no sight or sound of a plane. Rumors quickly spread through the crowd that there had been engine trouble and, possibly, an accident.

Half an hour later we heard the distant noise of an aircraft. It grew louder and louder, and soon an open-cockpit biplane appeared. It flew down the river toward the bridge, skimming just six inches above the water.

It was a scary sight!

As the plane approached the bridge, the tires occasionally nipped the water's surface, sending up nervous little splashes. I thought surely the water would grab the wheels and that the plane would go head over heels into the river, but it stayed aloft and zoomed through the narrow passage under the bridge. How that crowd roared!

But the crowd was disappointed when it was announced that this stunt had been performed by a stand-by pilot because Col. Springs's plane had indeed had engine trouble. Rumors again spread through the crowd that the colonel might have crashed.

Despite the enormous carrying power of politicians' voices in those times, we were too far away to hear a word of the formal bridge dedication. We hung around with the milling crowd while Dad enjoyed himself visiting the many friends he found. He took us over to speak to the governor of South Carolina, who patted both Oliver and I on the head. Then he turned to Dad and said: "Edwin, you have two fine looking boys."

In those days, governors made it an important part of their political business to know all the large landowners and farmers in the state, just as in later years they also made it their business to know the industrialists.

Dad introduced us to Col. Elliot's father, Leroy Springs. He occupied the high ground near the governors, the majors and their entourages.

We saw Dad's younger brother, Taylor, who was a dentist in Charlotte. We saw our cousin Henry Grady Hardin. His dad was a rising Methodist minister in Monroe, N.C., a city that would loom large in my later life.

We spoke to a fellow my sister Nancy had dubbed "Mr. Sausage" because he ran a sausage-processing plant near Charlotte and bought hogs from our dad.

We saw several of Dad's Jewish friends from Charlotte, who frequently came to our farm in Van Wyck to buy lambs and sheep. They were easy to recognize because they had full beards and wore black felt hats.

Two hours passed, and a large crowd still socialized by the river when we heard the noise of another approaching plane. It was the colonel himself, flying a dark gray, open cockpit biplane! It buzzed low over the bridge, then rose vertically in a precision Immelmann turn, executing a half-loop and rolling out on top to level flight.

Before anyone could draw a fresh breath, the plane dove straight for the river. Beside me, Oliver covered his eyes with his hands. I watched wide-eyed, frozen to the spot, my heart in my throat. Just as the nose of the plane was about to plunge into the river, it miraculously leveled off and zipped nonchalantly under the bridge! A woman behind me gasped in disbelief as the large crowd still standing on the banks erupted with cheers and thunderous applause. It took me a little longer to feel safe enough to let go of Dad's pants leg.

According to the picture on the next page, there weren't many people brave enough to witness Col. Springs's stunts from the actual deck of bridge.

Below the bridge, the plane turned back and, as if to make up for his late arrival, the colonel buzzed the bridge again, waving to the crowd while climbing in another breathtaking Immelmann. Then he leveled off and headed 10 miles south to his landing strip, back home in Fort Mill.

As the plane disappeared, the sound of the engine was replaced for a short while by the whine of cicadas along the riverbanks. A little later the noise rose again as hundreds of men cranked their cars and headed for home.

Back at our farm, mother greeted us.

"Hello, travelers. How was the show? It's nearly dark, I was getting worried about you. Edwin, did you have a flat tire?"

"No, we didn't have a flat," Dad answered. "We're late because

10

Col. Springs was two hours late, and the traffic coming home was heavier than I've ever seen."

We told Mother and my sisters, Nancy and Alice, all about our great adventure, the huge crowd, meeting lots of people, the governor and seeing two planes fly under the bridge.

With the makings of a prophet, I said to Mother, "Someday I want to fly!"

World War I ace Col. Elliot Springs zooms under the Buster Boyd Bridge near Charlotte, North Carolina, in July 1923. Mrs. Pettus, who as I write this is 97 and still lives in nearby Indian Land township, still talks about that exciting day. From her ancient scrapbook, she recently resurrected for me some newspaper clippings about the flight, along with this 73 year-old picture.

2
BARNSTORMERS & AIRMAIL PILOTS

My first airplane rides

On May 20, 1927, when I was 10 years old, my interest in flying and things mechanical peaked again when *The Charlotte Observer* announced: "Lindbergh flies non-stop from New York to Paris." This renowned event crowned my boyhood interest in mechanical contrivances and expanded my interest into the bigger world of aviation, an interest that has continued all my life.

Lindbergh's flight was even more remarkable when we remember that he designed significant features of the plane and helped build it in less than three months, working night and day with Ryan Aeronautical Co. engineers in San Diego. His plane was a major modification of an existing Ryan ship.

The Lindbergh plane was powered by a Wright air-cooled radial engine. It had a closed cabin, an all-aluminum body, a high monoplane wing —— all early innovations in the design of Ryan planes. Before this, most airplanes had open cockpits, fabric-covered wooden construction and were biplanes.

When Lindbergh flew "The Spirit of St. Louis" on its first shakedown flight, nonstop from its birthplace in San Diego to New York, he set a transcontinental speed record of 20 hours and 20 minutes. That was an omen of things to come. "Lucky Lindy" made his mark in aviation with the record-setting, 33-hour, nonstop solo flight of 3,000 miles across the Atlantic Ocean.

That daring trip rekindled my mother's memory of a remarkable event that had occurred 25 years before, when she was a freshman in college. She got out the encyclopedia and showed me the story about the Wright brothers and their first flight at Kitty Hawk, N. C., in 1903. On that historic day, they set three records for the longest

In 1927, Charles A. Lindbergh, an air-mail pilot, became the first person to fly non-stop across the Atlantic. His plane, the "Spirit of St. Louis," is on display today in the National Air and Space Museum in Washington, D.C.

-Library of Congress

flights, but for consid-e r a b l y lesser distances than Lindbergh: They flew 79 feet, 300 feet and 700 feet!

During the summer before that maiden flight, the Wright brothers had experimented with gliders, hopping into thermals created by stiff breezes blowing off the sand dunes at Kitty Hawk. At that time, the automobile was emerging in force. Henry Ford was racing and thinking about manufacturing his Model T, and numerous other inventors were building cars. So it was natural that the Wright brothers asked automobile companies for a quote on a special, light-weight engine that could be adapted for the first powered flight of their glider.

The car people declined.

The Wright brothers, not to be deterred from their ambitious plans, went back to their Dayton, Ohio, bicycle shop and designed and

The first powered flight of an aircraft -- the Wright Brothers at Kitty Hawk, North Carolina, Dec. 17, 1903

-Library of Congress

built their own engine, then used it to power the first flight of an airplane. This perseverance certainly illustrates the single-minded ambition the brothers had to possess to be the first to fly a powered aircraft.

I can only speculate that the car builders' interest was to construct engines bigger, heavier and with more horsepower. They weren't interested in maximizing the horsepower per pound of weight: the cardinal principle for the design of aircraft engines then and now.

There was another significant aviation milestone in 1927, the same year Lindbergh flew across the Atlantic for the first time: Amelia Earhart learned to fly. A month after Lindbergh's flight, she became a worldwide celebrity by accompanying a crew of three in a tri-motored Fokker across the Atlantic from Newfoundland to Wales in 21 hours. Later, in 1932, she was the first woman to pilot a red Lockheed Vega across the Atlantic. She and her navigator were lost without a trace in 1936 while attempting a flight across the Pacific.

At a dinner party on March 22, 1996, in Naples, Florida, I was talking with a friend, Cepe Smith, about this book. I was surprised to learn that his grandmother had lived on the same street with Amelia Earhart and her husband, publisher George Putnam. Cepe's Aunt Betty was a close friend of Amelia, and he remembered meeting her when the two families visited.

Cepe was only 6 years old when Amelia Earhart was reported missing.

"Aunt Betty was devastated when she heard her friend was reported missing; a broken friendship that I think affected her life thereafter," he told me. "I remember Miss Earhart as friendly and, in retrospect, not full of airs. I was aware that she was a pilot, but the full extent of her exploits she played down in her association with my family. We were, no doubt, a place of refuge from that world."

The year 1927 was big for aviation on another front. It was the year the federal government recognized the need to certify airplanes, and the "aircraft-type certificate" system that came to be called the ATC was enacted. All planes built after 1927 had to pass a government inspection for airworthiness and were given a type designation: the first, ATC #1, was an open-cockpit, fabric-covered biplane with a water-cooled engine. It was typical of the airmail and barnstormer planes of the mid-1920s.

In the late 1920s and early 1930s, as aviation flourished, barnstormers, bush pilots and mail carriers swarmed from fairgrounds, open pastures and grass landing strips. They went "wheels-up," and occasionally "noses-over," across the countryside, flying in an ever-developing variety of planes: Stearman biplanes with water-cooled, World War V12 Liberty engines, Ryan monoplanes and Stinsons with the new Pratt and Whitney Wasp radial engines. There was even a plane powered with a rear-mounted, Manasco in-line, six-cylinder engine, with a propeller that pushed rather than pulled.

Mail carriers criss-crossed the country, flying Wacos with OX5 V-8 engines. They usually got the mail through, but occasionally crashed when they strayed too far from the mountain passes and hit peaks in the Rockies that rose to altitudes higher than planes could fly. At great heights, the aircraft engines of those times couldn't take in enough air to maintain power. Of course, neither could the pilots. Pilots call them "nose-bleed" altitudes, the same name used by mountain climbers.

I n the fall of 1929, two years after Lindbergh's flight, my dad came home late from Waxhaw, N.C., one day and told me the town was buzzing with the story of a barnstormer who had

The Stearman Biplane

flown up and down the road between Waxhaw and Monroe, N.C., casing the area for a place to land. He found a flat, grassy pasture, but there were cows grazing on it. He circled a few times until he found an area with a fence on one side and trees on the other that appeared to be clear of cows and long enough to land on. So he slipped his plane in and bounced to a stop at the far side of the pasture.

The pilot removed his helmet and goggles, then clambered out. He found two large rocks and chocked the wheels. Then he drove two spikes into the ground and tied the plane down with lines running from the spikes to the ends of each wing. He stood there for several minutes and relaxed, noticing a nearby farmhouse. When he walked over, the pilot found the startled farmer who owned the field. The pilot explained that he wanted to rent the pasture for "hopping" passengers the next day, a Saturday. After some dickering, the farmer agreed to move the cows to another pasture and to rent the roadside field all day for $5.

The pilot strolled back to his plane, pulled out the sign he'd brought along and nailed it to a fence post beside the road:

FLY IN THE WACO BIPLANE

SEE YOUR FARM FROM THE AIR

$2.00

Then he walked three miles to Waxhaw, where he found and hired a strong boy, loafing at a service station, as his helper. The boy agreed to borrow his dad's car so he could make several trips to the service station the next day for gas, oil and water for the plane. The pilot bought his first stock of supplies, and the new helper gave him a lift back to the plane.

They refueled and oiled the plane, and topped off the radiator. The engine didn't have a self-starter, so the pilot briefed his helper on the most critical part of his job, "propping" the engine. With the ignition off, the propeller was pulled through the compression stroke several times to prime the engine. Then the pilot turned the ignition "on" and shouted "contact" as a warning to anyone who might be near the plane. The engine was started, or "cranked" as pilots say, by pulling the propeller briskly through the compression stroke again. The trick was to pull the propeller through hard, fast and

16

carefully, to step back quickly and to stand clear, and never to fall forward. The helper was put through the routine several times, and he caught on fast.

The pilot emphasized that the helper had to keep people away from the front of the plane because the engine would be left running, with the propeller turning, between flights. It would be stopped only for refueling.

The pilot settled in for the night under a wing of his plane.

Early Saturday morning, I biked over to the field, just across the North Carolina state line from our home in Van Wyck. I was now 12 years old and ready to spend the few dollars I had saved from my chores for a ride in an airplane. I had been dreaming about it ever since that day Col. Elliot Springs flew his stunts under the Buster Boyd Bridge.

The Waco biplane had three seats in tandem open cockpits. The pilot sat in the rear and the two passengers in front.

When I arrived I got a good look at the pilot, who had a deep tan and was wearing a helmet and goggles, with a silk scarf tied around his neck. Then I looked over that wonderful plane. It looked a lot like the one Col. Springs had flown, except that it was red and smelled like gasoline. The fabric covering on the wings was stretched so tightly that all the wooden ribs in the wing showed like the bones

A Waco biplane -- The barnstormer found a place to land.

in a starving cow. The wheels didn't have spokes: They were solid metal discs for better streamlining against the wind.

I bought a ticket and waited in line for my first ride.

The pilot's helper told me about arriving at the pasture just before sunup that morning with two egg-and-sausage sandwiches for the pilot's breakfast. He'd also brought supplies: two five-gallon cans of white, non-leaded gasoline, one gallon of oil, one five-gallon can of water for the plane, and a Mason fruit jar full of drinking water. Shortly after he arrived and they had serviced the plane, the boy collected $2 from each of the first two passengers and helped them aboard. He then propped the engine, and off they flew.

My turn came at last, and I climbed into the forward cockpit with another passenger. The plane quickly taxied to the fence at the edge of the pasture, turned and roared away toward the trees on the opposite side. We lifted off, and I thought we were going to take the tops of the trees at the edge of the pasture with us!

I tested the air by trying to raise my hand above the windshield, but the wind swept my arm back. I knew we must be flying at very high speed. Before I knew it, we were over Waxhaw. Henry Collins's livery stable, sitting on the town square next to Jessie Williams's bank, certainly looked different from the air. The mules milling about the barnyard and the people going in and out of the bank looked like little models. The crowd that always filled the sidewalks in the bustling farm town on Saturdays stopped, looked up, gawked and waved at the plane.

So many people were waiting for rides that the pilot didn't fly high enough or long enough to suit me. I was disappointed when we returned to the pasture so soon. We came in so hot, the skillful pilot had to side-slip the plane to lose speed and altitude before clearing the fence by inches, setting down in a three-point landing. He "greased it on," as they say. We rolled across the pasture and finally stopped just beneath the trees on the far side.

The plane was not only without an electric starter, it had neither flaps to slow the landing speed nor brakes to slow the ground speed. The pilot zig-zagged a lot to coax the plane to a stop before reaching the trees.

I had brought my lunch with me, and I ate with my cousin Harvey Morrison, son of a Coca Cola bottler from Monroe. I don't know how Harvey and his brother, Claude, got there so soon, but they never missed an event that drew a big crowd. They were busy peddling Cokes and hot dogs to the hungry and thirsty people.

The crowd was growing, and the helper was having trouble keeping curious onlookers away from the plane. He was too busy selling tickets and unloading and loading passengers, too busy to "prop" the engine after each flight. Late on Saturday afternoon, while two passengers were climbing out of the cockpit, the crowd moved in too close to the front of the plane and the spinning propeller. The pilot immediately shut off the engine and avoided what could have been a serious accident.

As darkness fell, the crowd cleared out. The helper took his last trip for fuel, oil and water. The pilot readied his plane for the flight out the next morning, paid his helper $1 and again slept under the wing. A dollar was a good day's wage in 1929, when farm hands were paid only 50 cents a day.

Later, I heard about the pilot's departure early Sunday morning: It seems that everybody in Waxhaw and Monroe knew every move the pilot made during his visit. They said the pilot had to prop the plane alone. He chocked the wheels with the same two stones and rotated the prop two revolutions to prime the engine. He hopped in the cockpit and switched on the magneto, set the throttle just above idling speed and, from force of habit, shouted "contact," even though nobody was around to hear him. He hopped back out again and vigorously pulled the prop through the compression stroke. The engine sprang to life, and the pilot hustled back into the rear cockpit. He fastened his seat belt and adjusted his goggles. Since there was nobody there to remove the chocks, the pilot advanced the throttle to full power and climbed the plane over them. He taxied to the fence, turned and took off over the trees.

The plane headed east into the rising sun. The pilot's next stop was Kitty Hawk, on the Outer Banks of North Carolina, where he would preside over another circus and spend the whole week hopping passengers.

My second chance to ride in an airplane came three years later, in 1932, when my uncle, Web White, the Shell Oil distributor in York County, put on an unusual promotion, especially for a "down-in-the-mouth" year in the middle of the Great Depression. He brought to Rock Hill, S.C., a seven-passenger Grumman Amphibian passenger plane to give his customers, both rich and poor, a ride in an airplane.

The Grumman Amphibian

The rides went on all day Friday, but the closest I got to the plane that first day was reading all about it in the *Rock Hill Evening Herald*. At noon on Saturday, while I was pumping gas at the local Shell service station, the manager breezed in from lunch and told me to hop in his car. He took me to the airport, and that blessed boss handed me a ticket for a ride in the Shell plane. He left me there and said I could take the rest of the day off! It was a VIP ticket, which meant it included a special flight that landed on Lake Wylie, north of Rock Hill.

The Amphibian didn't look anything like the barnstormer's open-cockpit biplane that had given me my first ride. This plane was a much bigger, closed cabin, high-winged monoplane with twin engines mounted side by side on top of the wings. The engines had to have electric starters because there was no place to stand on top of the fuselage to "prop" them.

The fuselage of the seven-passenger closed cabin hung below the wing. While it sat on the ground, the large front wheels of the landing gear extended below the fuselage, and the small tail wheel hung below a rudder that was used to guide the plane when it was on water. To land on water, the large front wheels were retracted to the upper side of the 'boat'.

Passengers climbed in from the top of the fuselage because the bottom was sealed so the plane could float. On water, the plane was further supported and stabilized with two pontoons that hung awkwardly from the ends of each wing.

I climbed up a ladder, stepped down into the cabin and found a good seat behind the two pilots. This airplane was "uptown" compared with the barnstormer's. There was no barrier between the pilots and the passengers, so I had a good view of everything the pilots did. I tried to understand the array of instruments on the large panel. I asked the captain if the craft was equipped for the "blind flying" I had read about in *Popular Mechanics*. He said this model wasn't rated for blind flying but, with a few more instruments, it could be.

The captain switched on the left electric starter, and the left-engine propellers slowly started to rotate. After picking up speed, the engine coughed and kicked and coughed again, then started, and the captain pulled back the throttle to idling speed. He repeated the procedure for the right engine, and it kicked and coughed and started.

We taxied to the end of the runway, and the pilot revved up each engine, checking the dual magnetos on each. The plane had variable-pitch propellers that improved efficiency at different engine speeds. He feathered each prop to be sure the hydraulic feathering system was functioning.

He looked back into the cabin and said, "Seat belts fastened?"

We took off and climbed over the residential and business areas of Rock Hill before heading for Lake Wylie, the large Duke Power Co. Reservoir between Rock Hill and Charlotte.

After circling the lake several times to be sure of a landing area clear of Saturday-afternoon boat traffic, the pilot flew down below the dam, then turned back toward the lake. The two large landing-gear wheels were retracted to wells in the fuselage near the top side of the cabin, well clear of the waterline after we landed. The pilot pulled back on the throttles and we glided down. He leveled the plane a few feet above the water and, as he continued to slow, the plane finally stalled and splashed in with a huge spray of water a hundred times bigger than my biggest watermelon dive.

We taxied for several miles, enjoying the curious stares from boaters and people sitting on the decks of their weekend cottages. After cruising for five or six minutes, the captain found another clear passage ahead, and he revved up the two big radial engines for take-off.

After a long run, leaving a deep wake behind us, the ship rose to the first step on the floating fuselage. After the out-rigged pontoons cleared the water, we quickly lifted off and became an airplane again. As we approached the airport at Rock Hill, the co-pilot lowered the landing wheels. When we landed, the plane bounced a little before the heavy front wheels and the trailing tail wheel settled to the ground. We climbed out and seven new passengers eagerly climbed in.

This amphibious, closed-cabin airplane, with its electric starters, flaps and brakes, was happy proof of how aviation was advancing during the late 1920s and early 1930s. And it definitely helped my love of flying do the same!

After that great plane ride, I loafed around the field for several hours watching the Amphibian land and take off every 15 minutes. The trip was longer when the plane landed on Lake Wylie.Late that Saturday afternoon, I caught a ride home with Uncle Web, who had spent the day at the field enjoying the loyalty of his oil customers.

When we got home, we saw a 1932-model Packard sedan parked in the driveway. When I recognized the chauffeur sitting in the driver's seat, I knew it belonged to my Uncle Jim, a wealthy retired doctor.

At the time, I was boarding with my dad's sister, Aunt Emma Lee, Uncle Web's wife. She had taken me in to finish the 11th grade in Rock Hill, where the school was better than in Van Wyck, to improve my chances of getting accepted at college.

"Uncle Jim and Aunt Beulah have driven over from Van Wyck to talk with you about college," Aunt Emma Lee said when we walked into the house.

I wondered what was up. After shaking hands with Uncle Jim and kissing Aunt Beulah, I said, "I just had a great ride in the Shell Amphibian plane this afternoon, and we landed on Lake Wylie. Maybe it's not too late for us to drive back out to the airport so you can have a ride. Uncle Web has extra tickets."

"Jim, I didn't come over here today to ride in an airplane," Uncle Jim said. "In fact, I will *never* ride in an airplane!" He looked very upset. "I have been waiting for you for more than an hour!"

Collecting himself, he got right to the point: "I have a serious plan for you to attend Duke University and study medicine. I'll pay all expenses and give you a generous allowance. When you graduate, I'll arrange for your internship at my old hospital in New York, and I'll help establish you in practice there."

I held my tongue, but felt like saying, "Don't you understand? I want'a fly airplanes!"

Fifteen years before this unexpected visit, when I was only one day old, Uncle Jim had taken a train from New York City to Van Wyck with an equally urgent plan for me on his mind. He came to my parents' home in search of the child that he never could have. Some years later, my mother told me about this visit from Uncle Jim.

"Give me a namesake: Name the newborn boy with Nisbet blood

James Douglas II. Fill my longing for a child that we could never have. I'll treat him as my own. He can live with us! We'll raise him, educate him, and he will be the heir to my estate," he'd pleaded with my parents.

How could the parents of a fourth son not seriously consider such a proposition from the wealthy great uncle? They agreed to name me after Uncle Jim, but they refused his request that I be given to him, and I thank them for that.

In 1925, when I was eight years old, Uncle Jim was suffering from heart trouble and had to give up his lucrative medical practice in New York City. He retired to his 2,000-acre estate in Van Wyck. Uncle Jim and Aunt Beulah had been in their 40s when they married, and they never had children.

The day of my Amphibian flight, I was only a few months shy of graduating from high school, and I had already been talking to my dad about going to North Carolina State and studying aeronautical engineering. My dad preferred that I take mechanical engineering at Clemson College, where tuition would be next to nothing for a resident of South Carolina.

Before Uncle Jim and Aunt Beulah left Rock Hill, I said to them, "I've told you before about my interest in flying and aviation. You must remember my excitement when Lindbergh flew the Atlantic. Surely you remember how I was bubbling over with enthusiasm after my first flight over Waxhaw with that barnstormer! And now you tell me this, just after I've had a ride in an Amphibian and landed on water!"

With all the moxie I could muster, I told Uncle Jim about my recent talks with my dad about college and my plans to study engineering. And I added, "I don't want to be a doctor!"

3

I LAND AT CLEMSON COLLEGE

My first solo flights

You guessed it. In the fall of 1933, I landed at Clemson College, now Clemson University, at the tender age of 16. In spite of all my disagreements with Uncle Jim, who had died the month before, Aunt Beulah was paying my way.

At Clemson, my interest in both engineering and aviation advanced even further despite the fact that my freshman year was disappointing. Clemson was a military college, and I didn't like being the butt of hazing, nor did I like ROTC, which consumed my time with training, discipline and demerits doled out just because

The Clemson Aero Club monoplane hangs above busy cadets in the South Carolina college's woodworking shop   -Clemson University Library

my room was dusty. Things got better during my sophomore year: I took a course in woodworking under Prof. Marshall, one of the most interesting teachers I ever had.

A few years before I arrived at Clemson, Prof. Marshall had formed the Clemson Aero Club. The club had designed, built and flown two airplanes, a biplane and a monoplane. The small monoplane hung from the ceiling of the woodworking classroom for all to see, admire and, of course, be distracted by.

How could any boy standing at those tables ever learn to chuck-up a piece of wood, turn it on a lathe and create a lamp when we all were enthralled by that beauty hanging from the ceiling?

In 1927 the state legislature lifted the ban on honorary societies with names composed of Greek letters, and the Clemson Board of Trustees ruled that professional and honorary organizations would be allowed to form chapters at Clemson.... About the same time, a group of students with an intense interest in airplanes organized the Aero Club, reputedly the first such organization at a southeastern college. The 10 original members, all of whom had some experience with airplanes before coming to Clemson, built a 17-foot biplane in the wood shop. The next year, club members emerged from the wood shop with a monoplane and had it checked and flown by professional pilots at the Greenville airport. The pilots thought the plane should have a larger engine, but it was well built. They particularly liked the position of the cockpit, which left the plane's balance independent of the pilot's weight.

At commencement in 1929, the Aero Club also flew a new glider that had taken them a scant three weeks to build. On a later flight the glider hit a tree and damaged the wing. Plans in October 1930 included repairing the glider and starting construction on a two-seater monoplane. By 1932, the club had acquired a wrecked Eaglerock biplane to repair and use for flying lessons, and a 120-hp Le Rhone engine for use as an experimental power plant. With such activities going on in the students' spare time, it was little wonder that the Engineering Department considered starting an aeronautical engineering program. The onset of money problems due to the Depression, however, held plans in check.

From Clemson University College of Engineering, One Hundred Years of Progress, 1989 *published by* **The Tiger.**

When the wood shop and foundry building was torn down a few years after I left Clemson, the little ship was moved to a museum in Columbia, S.C. I wondered if Prof. Marshall ever realized what a great gift he had left to posterity. It was a gift that has inspired and continues to inspire the imaginations of the young people who see the Clemson plane hanging at the museum, just as it hung from the ceiling in his classroom to inspire me.

The Clemson Aero Club's monoplane   -Clemson University Library

The club that had accomplished those unusual feats was disbanded in 1932 during the deepening Depression. My second year at Clemson, Prof. Marshall encouraged me to start a new flying club. He introduced me to a local army pilot named George who gave flying lessons in a Taylor Cub at the nearby Anderson airport. The Cub became better known as the Piper Cub when Taylor sold his interest in the company to Piper.

Back in the early 1930s, flying lessons were very expensive; I guess they still are. So I wrote my most appealing letter to Aunt Beulah, offering her the privilege of underwriting flying lessons as an important extracurricular activity for her favorite nephew and Uncle Jim's only namesake. To my relief, the dear lady agreed to sponsor me. She always was generous with me.

With the help of Prof. Marshall and the instructor, we organized a new Clemson flying club, and I became president. We always used

26

last names at Clemson, and I only remember the names of two of the six or eight club members, a senior named Barney and a freshman with the unforgettable name of Lindbergh.

Alarmingly, our instructor, George, liked his booze. All too frequently, he was tipsy when we flew with him. On one occasion, when I rode with him to the airfield, he went several miles off the normal route to an untraveled dirt road, pulling up in front of a farmer's dilapidated shack. The farmer came out and talked for several minutes. When he was satisfied that I was neither the law nor a stool pigeon, he took us behind the house and far out into a cotton field. There he dug up from his stash a Mason jar full of "white lightning." An even more descriptive name for the stuff was "rot-gut."

I must admit that, a few months later, I visited the same spot with my roommate and made a purchase for the Saturday night dance. On the following Sunday morning, I went to the infirmary rather than either church or to hide out on the river banks. It was "rot-gut" all right!

Believe it or not, George sometimes carried his flask of white lightning into the air during our instruction. He always ended his sessions with a snap roll and a loop, especially when he was "looped" himself. But he was a good pilot and instructor. I guess he thought I was a pretty good student because he let me solo in the Cub at the Anderson field after only two and a half hours of flight instruction. Today, the FAA requires at least 10 hours of airborne instruction before student pilots are allowed to solo.

We'd been making touch-and-go landings at Anderson for half an hour when George suddenly taxied to the edge of the field and climbed out.

"Okay, Jim, you're ready to solo. Take it around by yourself. I'm sure you can handle it!"

I was scared. I taxied out to the end of the runway and revved up the engine. I checked the dual magnetos by switching each one off. If the engine didn't quit, that proved both were functioning. (A redundant electrical system is required on all airplane engines.) I checked the fuel. The fuel gauge on the Cub was a calibrated rod with one end fastened to a cork floating in the fuel tank and the other end sticking up through a tube in the top of the fuel-tank cap. When a knob on the rod rested atop the cap, the tank was empty.

This made for a very effective gauge right in front of the windshield.

The only other instruments were a magnetic compass, oil temperature and pressure gauges, an altimeter and an engine tachometer. There was no air-speed indicator: The pilot had to judge the speed by the seat of his pants.

I taxied to the end of the active runway, lined the plane up for take-off and checked the magnetic compass to be sure it indicated a heading at least close to that of the runway.

Then I gave it full throttle, and I slowly picked up speed as the power took hold. I pushed the control stick forward to lift the tail off the ground and level the plane. When I felt the plane lighten and the controls become tighter but more sensitive, I knew I'd reached take-off speed. Picking up velocity, I eased back on the stick and the plane lifted off the ground.

I was flying!

I throttled back the engine from 2,500 to 2,000 rpm for climbing out. I leveled off at 1,500 feet, the proper altitude for circling the field and flying in the landing pattern.

When I started the first 90-degree turn to the right, it finally sank in that the front seat, where my instructor usually sat, was empty! I was alone! My hands got clammy; I started to sweat. Could I cut it? When I made the second 90-degree turn and leveled off on the downwind leg of the pattern, I looked to my right and spotted Barney, Lindbergh and our instructor watching from the ground. A third 90-degree turn put me on the base leg, and one more turn put me on final approach to the field.

I throttled back the engine to 1,500 rpm and started the descent. I glided in and, just past the threshold of the runway, I held the plane six inches off the ground until it stalled and I "greased it on." My buddies and George cheered!

The usual ritual after soloing would have been to cut off my necktie, but I wasn't wearing one, so they did the next best thing: They cut off my shirttail!

For several hours after I first soloed, I thought I was flying just as well as George, and I probably was because I was copying him. I thought I had it made and that there was nothing hard at all about flying. Then, for the next several hours, I couldn't do anything right. I couldn't make a decent turn, I couldn't hold altitude, I couldn't gauge the right glide path and the right altitude over the threshold of the runway. It got worse when I had to go around several times before landing because I didn't properly judge the headwinds. It took a lot more solo hours before I started learning to fly. Then I realized that the rule requiring 10 hours of instruction before soloing was a good idea.

After several of our club members had soloed in the Cub at Anderson, George bought a single-engine, two-cylinder, 36-horsepower Aeronca and moved our "circus" to a golf course that had been yet another victim of the Great Depression. It was more conveniently located, only a few miles from the Clemson campus.

The author "props" the Aeronca at its golf-course runway.

There were two big differences between the Cub and the Aeronca. The Cub's seating was tandem, with the student behind the instructor. Seating in the Aeronca was side-by-side; chummier it was. The control stick on the Cub was just a stick, but in the Aeronca it was a stick with a yoke at the end. Holding the yoke was much more comfortable: Like a Macintosh computer, it was "user friendly."

"Take it around by yourself," George suggested, after I'd spent only 30 minutes practicing touch-and-go landings in the Aeronca. This was his airplane, and if he trusted it with me so quickly, I had to be confident enough, or cocky enough, to solo and try to miss the sand traps when I landed.

I took off, made a climbing turn to the right, throttled back the engine to cruising rpm and leveled off. In this plane, the absence of the instructor in the right seat was not as obvious as in the Cub. After my second 90-degree turn put me on the downwind leg, I flew back by the golf course. When I looked down at the fairway on my right, I realized the length of the "landing strip," this golf-course fairway, was very short compared with the long runways at the Anderson airport.

About a mile past the golf course, I turned 90 degrees on the base leg for a short time, then turned on the final leg in the landing pattern, cut power to 1,500 rpm and started the descent. The golf course was in plain sight straight ahead. The fairway looked so short that I had real doubts about whether I'd make it in. But I managed to set the Aeronca down on the fairway, even though I didn't quite "grease it on." I rolled on until the little toy airplane stopped at a distance not much farther than I can drive a golf ball on a good day.

My first long-distance flight was to be a weekend trip home in the Aeronca with my roommate. Our instructor wasn't keen on all the FAA rules, so he didn't mind if I flew with a passenger. But I was supposed to have a private license to do that. If we had an accident, the instructor's insurance company, if he even had one, almost certainly wouldn't pay up.

We topped the tanks from the five-gallon can of white, non-leaded gasoline we had bought at the filling station near the field. George propped the engine. Like the Cub, the Aeronca didn't have brakes or a self-starter.

Just before we took off, George bid us a safe voyage and said, "By the way, Jim, you should circle the golf course and gain some altitude before leaving the area."

I took off and followed his advice by flying west until we reached 2,000 feet. Then I made a 180-degree turn eastward and set the compass course to fly back across the golf course before heading over the woods. Our destination was half way across South Carolina. By the time I crossed back over the golf course, I was at the comfortable altitude of 2,500 feet.

Then the engine stopped!

To avoid stalling and a sure spin, I lowered the nose at once. Fortunately, we had practiced cutting the engine and had simulated forced landings. Next, I established a glide path to keep the plane flying in an eerie silence without an engine. After turning back 180 degrees downwind and establishing a landing pattern, I had to make a critical judgment of distance and timing before turning back toward the golf course, then gliding at the right angle to meet the threshold of the fairway. I managed, and we landed safely.

Once on the ground, with an Olympic-sized sigh of relief, I let her roll free and, sure enough, we came to an abrupt stop in the middle of a sand trap. At least that was better than the middle of a forest! George was still hanging around. He'd watched the entire flight, so by no means did I begrudge him the chug-a-lug he took from his flask as he approached the plane. I will be forever grateful to that man for the advice that probably saved our lives that day.

During my junior year at Clemson, Prof. Fernow hired me as his lab assistant. The work involved setting up experiments for the engineers' lab classes, and to do that I got to know steam engines, steam turbines, auto and aeronautical engines and all the related gauges and instruments that went with them.

When the good professor asked me to think about a project for the college's upcoming Engineering Week, I immediately thought of the V-12 World War I Liberty engine that I had been eyeing as it sat in a basement hallway. I corralled Barney and Lindbergh, and we got the professor's approval for our project: To mount the Liberty engine on a test stand outside the Earl Engineering Building and try to run it during engineering week.

Luckily for us, the engine had come to the college with its own test stand or operating bed. With a load of advice from Prof. Fernow and help from the school's maintenance department, we mounted this 1,000-pound relic on the test bed in a valley below the engineering building.

The compression stroke on this engine was too great for it to be started by normal "propping," so the electrical system had an advanced sparking procedure. We still had to prime the thing by jumping off the ground and catching the horizontal end of the 12-foot propeller, then riding it down several times through the compression cycle. Then one blade of that prop was set just beyond the lower vertical position, the ignition switch was turned "on" and the prop was pulled two feet against the compression stoke opposite the running direction, then released. When the prop rebounded in the running direction, the advanced ignition fired and the engine roared to life with the loudest noise ever heard before or since on the normally quiet Clemson campus.

During this hair-raising maneuver, I was on the stand manning the throttle. I was startled not only by the noise but also by the stand, which started to slide forward with the pull of the propeller. I shut the engine down, and we had to tether the test frame to a large oak tree a few yards behind before starting the engine again.

The engine drank so much gas that we couldn't buy enough to disturb the peace for very long on that first day. On the second day, soon after we started our noise machine, the president of the college declared that the racket was shutting down everything else on campus, so he shut *us* down. We had run out of money for gas anyway.

Prof. Fernow declared that we'd done the mechanical engineers proud.

P rofessors Fernow and Sams, both in the Mechanical Engineering Department, boosted even more my interest in flying and my enthusiasm for the Liberty engine project.

Prof. Sams lectured about the inability of internal combustion engines to maintain power in the rarefied air at high altitudes. He said that one solution was the supercharger. This handy device could feed compressed air directly into the carburetor and, at 20,000 feet, fool the engine into thinking it still was operating at sea level.

This led Prof. Sams to his fascinating lectures about engineering prospects beyond the supercharger: the gas turbine. It would combine the virtues of the supercharger with the internal combustion engine and could maintain sea-level power at high altitudes.

In the 1930s, engineering theories were well advanced for designing gas turbines, and they awaited only the further development of closer tolerances in manufacturing and the evolution of metals that could maintain strength at high temperatures. The efficiency of gas turbines is directly related to the turbine's operating temperature: the hotter the better, like red hot, between 1,200 and 1,500 degrees.

Our flying club persuaded Prof. Sams to add a course in aeronautical engineering to the mechanical engineering curriculum. We argued that if we couldn't build our own airplane, we should at least have a course about aviation. As we'd learned from the Clemson Aero Club a few years before, the promotion of an aeronautical course was not a new idea.

In that wonderful course we learned about things like "lift" and "drag." For example, we learned that if the drag of the landing gear is removed by retracting the gear into the fuselage, the plane can fly 10 to 15 percent faster with the same horsepower. Such is the case with the modern, retractable-gear Cessna 210.

The Cessna 210

When it came to retractable landing gear, Wiley Post was an early pioneer. He also was one of the first pilots to experiment with a pressurized suit and one of the first to test the General Electric Moss turbo supercharger.

In 1931, Post, flying a Lockheed Vega named Winnie May, with Harold Gatty as his navigator, set a round-the-world speed record of eight days, 15 hours and 51 minutes. I imagine that while he was flying over thousands of miles, across mountains and oceans, he must have realized that the landing gear hanging beneath him was an impediment to his progress.

When he got home, Post decided to do something about it. He designed a system for dropping the landing gear after take-off, and when he adapted the idea to his Lockheed Vega he proved his point by winning all the races, at least until other racers caught on.

But Post still had to land when he got home. This problem was easily solved by landing on metal skids mounted on the bottom of the fuselage.

They say all flyers of retractable landing-gear planes either already have or soon will land "wheels up." But I know that isn't always true because I asked my technical consultant for this book, Bruce Bowers, a TWA pilot who flew a Boeing 747, if he ever had landed without lowering the gear, and he said, "I haven't yet."

But we won't worry about Bruce landing his 747 "wheels up." He retired last year.

Wiley Post wasn't so lucky. He was killed on a flight to Russia in 1933. His passenger was the renowned humorist of the time, Will Rogers.

During the summer following my junior year, my older brother, John Ed, was working as the soil conservationist in Lancaster County, S.C. He gave me a job driving a bull-dozer, building terraces for farmers as part of President Franklin D. Roosevelt's conservation program. That job involved more sitting than working, thanks to the never-ending problem of air locks in the early Diesel engine that powered the Caterpillar tractor. The frustration of dealing with that beast almost killed my interest in all things mechanical!

John Ed was interested in flying, and he wanted me to take him up for a ride. Telling him that without a private license I wasn't qualified didn't cut any ice with him. So one Sunday morning we drove to the Charlotte airport, known then as Morris Field and not much bigger than a pasture. Luckily, I found a pilot there who owned an Aeronca, the same kind I flew at Clemson. I flashed my log book and student permit and asked the owner if I could rent his plane for an hour or two. He said he would check me out and see.

We took off, and I made two touch-and-go landings, which satisfied the fellow. We taxied in, the owner climbed out, and I beckoned John Ed to climb in. The pilot looked a little skeptical but didn't stop us.

John Ed was a great outdoorsman and wanted to see his fishing domains from the air. We flew at 1,000 feet, down the Catawba River to Columbia, where it becomes the Santee River, then down to where it becomes the Cooper River, north of Charleston.

On the return trip, we circled our house and waved to the family, which that day included our Uncle Taylor and his brood, who had come by for one of their frequent Sunday-afternoon visits.

Dad told me later that after we had flown away, Uncle Taylor had said, "Edwin, it looks like Jim might be as wild as I was when I attended Clemson a long time ago."

4

WHEELS UP FOR GENERAL ELECTRIC

My private license and first commercial flights

One spring morning in 1937, during my senior year at Clemson, I was catapulted from college to a career. It was an exciting day for every senior in engineering because a recruiter from General Electric had arrived to interview the engineering graduates. A job offer from GE was considered the top prize for an engineer. My sponsors, professors Fernow, Sams and Marshall, spoke up for me, and apparently I didn't spoil things during my interview.

A few weeks before, I'd received an appointment to the Naval Air Corps from Jimmy Burns, U.S. senator from South Carolina. I passed the rigorous physical examination with the critical eye test, and was accepted.

Now I faced a decision: Accept my appointment in the Naval Air Corps and a career in aviation, or go to work for GE as a student engineer. The Air Corps would allow me to pursue my love of flying, but the GE job seemed a greater challenge and an opportunity for a broader career.

I talked it over with Dad.

"Jim, I think you should take the student engineering job at GE. In a year or two, if you still want to go to the Naval Air Corps, you can, and you'll have a broader engineering education that'll be of great value in anything you might want to do later," he explained.

"Okay, Dad, that settles it, but I don't have the money to get to Schenectady. It's someplace way up there in northern New York."

Dad figured that since I had graduated, I was on my own. I argued that since I was only 20, I still had a year to go before I reached adulthood. He took me to the bank in Waxhaw, the same bank I had flown over in my first flight with the barnstormer. Jessie Williams, the bank president, gladly loaned me $100 on a 90-day note as soon as he learned that my dad would co-sign it.

I was surprised that paying off that $100 note at $30 a month from my $112-a-month GE paycheck was such a burden. I'd forgotten that I had to replace my Clemson military wardrobe with "civilian" clothes. And, for the first time in my life, I had to pay for my own room and board.

On top of this, insurance salesmen seemed to have the names of all student engineers before they arrived at Schenectady, and they told convincing stories about the hazards of our jobs. I remembered that tenant farmers back home had burial insurance, and some had coffins laid away. Deciding that prudence was the better part of valor, I bought both life and accident policies, paying in advance from my shrinking treasury.

At 7:30 on the rainy Monday morning of June 21, 1937, I left my boarding house in Schenectady, walked down State Street and turned left on Erie Boulevard toward the towering lights of the GE monogram above Building #2 in the Schenectady works. I was reporting for my first day of work as a student engineer.

My first assignment was testing industrial control equipment. I worked the second shift, from 3 p.m. to midnight, so my mornings were free. I joined the Edison Club, which was subsidized by GE, and the company paid the dues. The Edison Club was, of course, named after the famous Thomas A. Edison, inventor of the electric light bulb, phonograph and many other things, and one of the founders of GE.

The normal "test" assignment at GE was three months. When my first assignment ended I wasn't sorry to pack my trunk and leave Schenectady for a motor-generator test assignment at a plant in Ft. Wayne, Indiana.

The three-month assignment in Ft. Wayne passed quickly even though it, too, become repetitive during the last few weeks. I was ready to pick up and move to another assignment. This time it was "steam turbines" at Lynn, Massachusetts, near Boston.

The giant steam turbines were too complicated and expensive to be trusted solely to inexperienced test men, so GE had permanent test men who supervised the student engineers. During the last month of this assignment, I worked as a draftsman for one of these supervisors.

My three months at Lynn ended quickly, and I was ready to move on because I didn't want to be stuck at a drawing board in the engineering office. I'd learned to enjoy that nomad's life and a new stand every three months.

With my trunk packed again, I was off to Bloomfield, New Jersey, across the Hudson River from New York City. The work there was testing air-conditioning equipment in a development lab. It was a very pleasant three months, with a congenial roommate and New York City nearby. My roommate and I spent more than we earned, though I don't know how we did that in those days before credit cards.

Another three months came and went, and the assignment added another chapter of industrial product to my book of knowledge about GE's output. I was disappointed that I hadn't found a product related to aviation.

I left the busy and buzzing New York area for sleepy and quiet Pittsfield, Mass., where GE built electrical transformers. These weren't the little ones that hang on utility poles outside many houses in the city and countryside, but big ones, some as large as a modern living room. We had to climb into these things and clean them, and it was the grimiest job you ever can imagine. To make matters worse, I was on the "graveyard shift": midnight to 8 a.m., and with the Great Depression still under way, we worked only two or three days a week.

I learned for the first time what it means to be an hourly paid worker without much work. To this day, when I read about layoffs in industrial plants, I feel for those hourly workers, especially ones with families to feed.

I complained enough about the lack of work to be transferred from Pittsfield back to Lynn, Mass., and an assignment at the Thompson Laboratory (named after a prominent electrical engineer) in an entirely different field, metallurgy, something that turned out to be closely related to aviation.

Before accepting this offer, I had my last interview with John Borring, the man who had hired me back at Clemson. Borring told me that during his many years at GE, he had observed that engineers frequently made faster progress when they changed fields, away from that of their formal education: from mechanical engineering to electrical, from electrical to chemical or, in my case, from mechanical engineering to metallurgy.

"All engineering education has basic disciplines applicable to all branches, but changing to one outside one's degree field inspires greater curiosity, less confidence and an extra effort to catch up. Frequently, this puts one ahead," Borring said.

This was similar to the advice my dad had given me when I wanted to attend North Carolina State and study aeronautical engineering. He suggested Clemson and mechanical engineering. Again, when I was leaning toward that appointment to the Naval Air Corps, he urged that I go to GE first and get an advanced education in engineering.

Borring cinched the case for my move to Lynn when he told me about Dr. Moss, the inventor of the supercharger, who worked at the Lynn plant. The supercharger is an air compressor driven by exhaust gases that enables an airplane's internal combustion engine to maintain sea-level horsepower at high altitudes.

In June 1918, Moss tested his supercharger atop Pike's Peak, proving that a 350-horsepower Liberty engine could maintain sea-level horsepower at 14,019 feet. However, the test also showed that the turbine wheels and blades had to run at red-hot temperatures for the supercharger to perform efficiently. While running red hot for a long time, the blades stretched so much that they lost their shape. Therefore, the useful life of the supercharger was limited by the lack of strength of even stainless steel, the best known high-temperature alloy at the time.

"During the past year, I've recruited only two metallurgists, and I need more if we're going to develop the supercharger. The head of the Thompson Laboratory wants another student engineer to work with the chief metallurgist, Bill Badger, to develop better high-temperature alloys by working with special steel companies," Borring explained.

"The field is so new that there isn't any such thing as a graduate in high-temperature metallurgy," he hastened to add.

I accepted the mantle of metallurgical trainee and was off again to Lynn to study and practice in this new field.

During my first year at the Thompson lab, I read and studied all the metallurgy textbooks my colleagues had studied at the Virginia Polytechnic Institute. This homework, plus daily experience in the discipline, put me in a competitive position with my few peers who had graduated in metallurgy, just as Borring had predicted.

The extra effort proved well worth it. Soon I was rewarded with a permanent job as a metallurgist in the Thompson lab, and I was assigned to help develop high-temperature alloys for steam turbines and superchargers, a most interesting and challenging job and the basis for a later business career.

In 1940, war clouds darkened the horizon. The U.S. government secretly brought Sir Frank Whittle, a British engineer and one of the inventors of the gas turbine, to America to help develop the gas turbine for aircraft propulsion. Sir Frank lived in the home of Reginald Standardwick, the chief engineer at the General Electric supercharger plant. He stayed for the duration of the war, collaborating with GE engineers. Late in the war, they together built the first U.S. gas turbine to power the first jet-propelled fighter plane.

This was the same type of engine Prof. Sams had spoken to us about during my Clemson days. It held great promise for replacing both the internal-combustion engine and the turbo supercharger for aircraft propulsion, and this came to be called jet propulsion. I remember seeing Sir Frank, that mysterious house guest of our chief engineer, slipping around, conferring with the senior engineers and my boss, the chief metallurgist, who finally introduced me to him.

I became very fond of Boston and New England. I sailed, skied, partied and courted New England girls. I lived in a co-op house with seven other GE engineers, in a nice, quiet residential neighborhood in Marblehead, a half-block from the ocean.

Conservative New England neighborhoods didn't relish the company of young men who lived in co-op houses. For example, during our first winter we had a snowstorm, and Bill Macintosh, one of our big Texas A&M boys, was shoveling the snow from our driveway. The lady next door, whom we had never met, came out and shouted at him:

"Don't you throw any snow on my property!"

"Wait 'til you're hit before you holler, lady!" Bill yelled back

After a vain search for students interested in flying, I joined a sailing partnership with two other fellows. We bought a 32-foot sloop. We were pure sailors: Our sloop had no auxiliary engine, only sail or rowing power. Our partnership also had rigid written rules. One banned alcoholic beverages aboard.

One Saturday afternoon, we were sailing about 30 miles north of

Boston and several hundred yards off Manchester when the wind suddenly died. The sails flopped about, and it looked as though we might have to drift all night. An hour before dark, Janice Halverson (the prettiest member of our six-person crew that day) and I rowed ashore in the dinghy we always towed behind the boat. The Massachusetts shore is rocky and deep, and we almost swamped several times before docking. We finally got ashore below a huge mansion on the hill above.

We walked to the back of the house and told the couple who met us of our plight, becalmed without food or water. They accepted us graciously, invited us in and said they had watched us sail — or try to sail — our sloop for two hours. It was cocktail hour for the couple, and they invited Janice and me to join them for two strong martinis while their maid fixed us a large box of food and drink for what was shaping up to be an overnight stay on the sloop.

The earlier problem of getting ashore had been bad enough. Now we had to get back aboard. Standing on a rock and trying to board the dinghy, which was bobbing about three feet up and down with the incoming waves, was almost impossible. Exasperated, we finally just hurled our food into the boat and leaped in ourselves as the boat rose to the top of an incoming wave. Luckily, we didn't swamp. Back aboard the sloop, Janice and I opened our box of loot to find a variety of goodies, including a bottle of rum. One of our persnickety partners invoked the rules and declared the rum could not be opened.

The sails flopped all night, and Janice and I kept the late-hour watch, with the unopened rum. Our boat did not have a "head," known to landlubbers as a toilet, so at sunup we found relief with a refreshing swim. About 10 a.m., a 20-knot breeze sprang up, and we sailed home at last.

The thrill of sailing in a brisk breeze is unforgettable: sliding through the water with the boat keeled over at 20 degrees, the waves lapping against the rails of the deck, watching the billowing "mains'l," the taut jib, the tight sheets, and feeling the pull of the tiller. After sailing home and shouting a final "ready about," I headed the vessel into the wind. It stopped dead still just as I reached out and grabbed the buoy where we moored the boat off the beach at Swampscott. After cleaning the boat, Janice, my sweetheart now, and I commandeered the rum, and we had another rendezvous that night with an opened bottle.

Janice was a senior at Simons College in Boston. I had written my mother about her, and Mother's response was to invite her to South Carolina for a visit. We drove down and had a delightful time. I believe Janice would have married me in a minute, but I wasn't ready to take that big step.

It was during this stand at Lynn that I had my first chance to fly again. Congress, anticipating World War II, established the Civilian Pilots Training Corps, which became known as the CPTC. The purpose was to attract 18- to 24-year-old volunteers to take free, government-sponsored flying lessons for 40 to 50 hours and, if successful, to graduate with a private pilot's license.

I applied with two friends from GE, Frank Bruno and Jack Adamson, whom I'd boarded with during my first job in Schenectady and who now were in Lynn.

The CPTC training planes were four-cylinder, 65-horsepower, two-passenger tandem Piper Cubs, the standard plane for pilot training for many years. This was a slight step up from my earlier flying experience in the 50-horsepower Cub and the two-cylinder, 30-horsepower Aeronca at Clemson. I'd had only about 15 hours of solo flying at Clemson, but that was enough for me to quickly complete the minimum 35 hours required by Uncle Sam and to pass both the written and flight tests for a private pilot's license.

An advanced program in acrobatics was offered to the "cream of the crop" graduates from the first phase of the program. Bruno, Adamson and I all were selected for the advanced program. Only Bruno accepted, and he went on to learn all the stunts: loops, barrel rolls, wing-overs and Immelmann turns. When America entered the war a year later, Bruno was drafted, and I never again heard from him or many other friends who met the same destiny.

Jack Adamson and I turned down the advanced program because we saw the war clouds growing too thick for comfort. That was a third decision that no doubt had a big effect on my destiny and prevented me from getting involved in World War II. I was never commissioned a second lieutenant and was not called to serve during World War II. Looking back, my repeated rejection of chances to fly when I loved to fly so well are hard to fully explain.

I was deferred throughout the War in a "vital to industry" classification. I was never a soldier. In fact, I loathed the idea of being a soldier, and I guess I gave up opportunities to fly to avoid being a soldier. Maybe Clemson's military rules and the rigid demerit system had something to do with it.

On December 20, 1940, I took my first commercial flight on Eastern Airlines, in one of those venerable old DC3s. I stood at the gate, I think it was the only gate, at Logan Field in Boston (now a huge international airport), and I watched the DC3 land. It taxied in and, when it approached the gate, the pilot revved up the left engine, pushed the right rudder forward, braked the right wheel, and the plane turned to the right and stopped. A line boy rushed out and put chocks under the front wheels, then walked to the rear of the plane and opened the small passenger door. He put a stool beside the plane opposite the door and the first passenger stepped out.

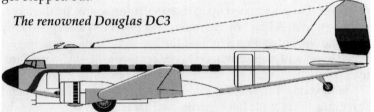

The renowned Douglas DC3

When everyone had debarked, the line boy opened a larger door just forward of the tail and unloaded a few pieces of luggage and a small sack of mail. Then he loaded fresh luggage and fresh mail before beckoning for the departing passengers to clamber aboard.

When I climbed inside the DC3, I was impressed by the size of the cabin. It was a lot bigger than the seven-passenger Grumman I had ridden in 1932. The 26 seats were arranged with a row of single seats to the left of the aisle and a row of double seats to the right. As soon as I stepped inside the plane, I noticed the floor was not level but was inclined toward the front of the plane at an angle about like that of a wheelchair ramp. The DC3 was a "taildragger." I walked forward, up the inclined floor, to a seat near the front and just behind the pilot's cabin. When I sat down and fastened my seat belt, I could feel that the seat was not level. Naturally, I was disappointed that the single flight attendant was a young man.

After all the passengers were settled and the rear door was closed, the captain started the left and then the right engines. We taxied a very short distance to the active runway and stopped. He separately revved up each engine to full power, checked the dual magnetos and test-feathered the variable-pitch propellers.

We taxied onto the runway. After full power was applied and we had rolled a few hundred feet, the control yoke was pushed forward to raise the tail. When we had picked up flying speed, the pilot pulled back on the control wheel and we took off for a bumpy ride south. The DC3 was not pressurized nor were the engines supercharged, so we couldn't fly any higher than 12,000 feet. We must have traveled through a weather front before we reached New York, our first stop, because it was a very turbulent and unpleasant ride.

The plane stopped in New York, Washington, Richmond and Raleigh before arriving, nearly eight hours later, in Charlotte. Eastern was the only airline that served Charlotte at the time, with two flights a day. The plane landed in Charlotte about dusk. There was no control tower. The pilot taxied up to the small tarmac area by the three-room terminal. A line boy came out and put the one-step stool by the rear door, only about a foot off the ground, for the passengers. I stayed overnight at my boyhood home across the line in South Carolina.

The next day, I flew on to Miami, because I was going to spend Christmas there with Janice, who had taken a job a few months before as a clerk at a small Miami Beach hotel. After landings in Columbia, Savannah and Jacksonville, I arrived just before dark in Miami. It was another long day of flying at 150 mph at the uncomfortable, bumpy altitude of 10,000 to 12,000 feet.

Janice met me and, before I flew away on Sunday morning, the great, two-year romance that had begun on that 32-foot sloop ended on Miami Beach. I lost my first love, my beautiful, extremely well proportioned girlfriend to a middle-aged man who had enticed her to be his front-desk clerk. I neither saw nor heard from her again, but I have thought of her a thousand times.

A year later, on December 7, 1941, I was having a very late breakfast with two or three housemates at our "den of wolves" in Lynn when we heard the news on the radio: Pearl Harbor had been attacked.

All but two of our seven housemates at the time were ROTC reserve officers. They had gone to military schools and had received reserve commissions as second lieutenants. Before the week was out, they were all called for active duty: gone; leaving only two of us to close the house and try to get out of our year's lease.

With America at war, GE built a new plant in Ft. Wayne for the mass production of superchargers. I was asked to be chief metallurgist there, and I accepted in 10 seconds. Nothing was left for me in Boston except fond memories of Janice Halverson. A few weeks later, I was on my way for a second tour of duty in Indiana.

I got there in my new, brown, two-door 1941 Ford V8, which I was able to buy with a loan from my mother. It was one of the last cars off the assembly line until 1946, after the war ended.

I stopped to spend two days with my parents in Van Wyck, S.C., not exactly on the way to Indiana. I will always revel in my memories of that visit because I saw my dad alive only one more time.

Dad and I talked a lot about "what-ifs." What if I had continued in ROTC at Clemson and was now an Army officer? What if I had gone to the Naval Air Corps and was now a flying officer in the Navy, and what if I had taken the advanced CPTC course? They're questions that never will be answered. I appreciated the fact that my dad's advice to me was the reason I was at GE rather than in the military. My career was heading toward the manufacture of aviation equipment in support of the war effort.

When Dad said, "Jim, now that you're a private pilot, what are you going to do about flying?"

"When I save enough money, I'll buy an airplane," I replied.

5

THE SHADOW
OF WORLD WAR II

My first airplane

A wartime climate quickly settled over the United States and particularly over the supercharger plant in Ft. Wayne, Indiana. We worked six days a week. Superchargers had to be mass produced and shipped to fly in combat planes over Europe and the Pacific. Early in the war, the best high-temperature alloys available were marginal, so they limited the supercharger's useful life. The job pressure never let up.

Most guys my age had gone off to war. I was classified "vital to industry," deferred for the war effort at home.

Soon after I arrived in Ft. Wayne, Ed Mathews, an engineer at the plant, took me to the home where he roomed and boarded. It was a large house on the outskirts of town and only a half-mile walk from our work. The place was owned by Claire and Page Yarnell, a prominent Ft. Wayne couple. Their oldest son was married and lived next door on their five-acre compound. Their three oldest daughters were married to young GE engineers who had once enjoyed room and board with the Yarnells. The youngest daughter, Agnes, attended Antioch College in Ohio. I accepted their invitation to move in and share a room with Ed Mathews.

The Yarnells were patrons of the arts. Claire, the matriarch of the clan, stayed up every night until the wee hours reading the books she would review on Sunday for the *Ft. Wayne Sentinel*.

I joined the family for every performance of the Ft. Wayne Symphony, where the Yarnells always had the best seats in the house. Page, the patriarch, was a partner in a large wholesale hardware company, Mossman-Yarnell. He was a generous and lovable man. I guess one could say I became "thick" with the Yarnells.

Behind their house was a large lake that froze over in the winter, and when Agnes was home from school, she taught me how to ice skate. I had read in *Readers Digest* that the best way to learn to skate was to first learn how to fall. I had fun learning how to fall down with Agnes, and eventually discovered how to skate, backwards too. Sure enough, some six months later, Agnes and I were engaged.

Mother and my sister, Nancy, came from South Carolina for the wedding. Mother told me later that they didn't feel at home with my new in-laws.

Page loaned me the money to buy a nice little house outside town, and he gave me a half-inch portable drill when I quickly started some remodeling.

Agnes and I were married for only five months. I thought I was making some rather substantial adjustments to married life, but I knew it was not going smoothly.

I came home from work one Saturday afternoon and noticed that the morning paper was still in the driveway. I wondered why. I found Agnes sitting in a chair by the dining room table, with a packed suitcase beside her. The table was bereft of dinner. I had the feeling she had been sitting there all day long. She must have been reluctant to call her mother or her dad, or perhaps she was just waiting to tell me "goodbye."

When she said she was leaving, I was dumbstruck, angry and totally unable — or unwilling — to understand her feelings. Our magnified emotions filled the room. I suggested that she call her dad to come and pick her up. She did, and he promptly appeared at our house, totally misreading the scene.

"Isn't it wonderful, Agnes, you must be pregnant!" he chirped.

There was a long silence, and I said, "Page, Agnes has made certain she is not with child."

This was followed by several months of unsuccessful attempts at reconciliation by her parents, her brother, her sisters and by me. All the while, I was reading Carl Mininger's book, *The Human Mind*, looking for some handles to hold. Only two months later, Agnes's cousin, a lawyer, arranged for a divorce by charging "cruel and inhuman treatment!"

"Indiana law, you know!" he said.

"You S.O.B., you know," I replied.

I remembered that, a few weeks before our wedding, Page had asked me, "Jim, are you and Agnes really in love?"

This was my first worrisome clue that our affection for each other might be wanting. That was when I was trying to figure out what love was.

At this crossroads in my life, the only escape I could think of was to buy a plane and fly again. I was restless. I needed to commune with the heavens again, to work out causes and effects, to be able to fly and dodge the cumulonimbus clouds. I wanted to visit my mother in South Carolina, whom I hadn't seen since traveling there for my dad's funeral a few months before.

During World War II, fuel for cars was rationed, but, believe it or not, fuel for private flying wasn't. I met an engineer who had soloed and another who was interested in learning to fly. We formed a partnership and went looking for an airplane. We found a neat Luscomb, a two-seater and one of the first all-aluminum, single-engine planes. We couldn't come up with the $4,000 the owner wanted, so we settled on a Stinson Voyager for $3,200, which fell almost within our budget of $1,000 each, so we stretched and bought it.

The Stinson Voyager -Collection of the Author

The Stinson was a closed-cabin, three-seater, high-wing, fabric-covered monoplane, powered by an 85-hp Continental engine. We thought it was particularly nifty because it had flaps, a self-starter, and it was red. We stationed our new toy at the Warsaw airport, about 20 miles from Ft. Wayne.

My first cross-country experience flying the Stinson took place on a sunny weekend in the spring of 1943. I was very tired of working on Saturdays week in and week out, and it seemed as though the war would never end. When I left for work one Saturday morning in June, at 7:30 on a beautiful spring day, I couldn't resist the temptation to "play hooky," and I went to the airport rather than to work.

I took off in the Stinson and headed for South Carolina.

This was an 800 mile, 10-hour hop. After two fuel stops and a long day of flying in bumpy weather, I finally arrived, just before dark, over my home in Van Wyck. I buzzed the house, and my mother and sister, Nancy, came out, completely astonished, and waved. I throttled back the engine and circled low over the house again, shouting down for them to meet me in Lancaster, which had the nearest airport. They understood, and a few minutes later I landed in Lancaster. Mother and Nancy pulled up and greeted me soon after I arrived.

"Son, what in the world ever possessed you to fly all the way from Indiana all by yourself?" Mother asked.

"I got homesick."

My dad didn't live long enough to see my first plane, but I remembered all of his good advice to me along the way. I'm sure he would have been pleased to see me flying as a hobby rather than as a livelihood.

Nancy's husband was fighting in the Pacific. Fortunately, she was teaching in nearby Monroe, and lived with Mother during her first years without our dad. Having someone at home, to start and end the day with, was a great comfort to Mother during the first difficult years without "Edwin."

A few months before I returned for this brief visit, an auctioneer had successfully disposed of all the farm equipment, and that was depressing because Mother always enjoyed seeing the mules leave the barn at daybreak and return at dark after a long day plowing in the fields. The sale meant that farming on "Mr. Ed's" land had come to a close.

I wanted to stay a week or two rather than only one night, but I didn't share Mother's sadness over the end of the farm: The era had passed. I told Mother that I thought my older brother, Oliver, would return from the war in Europe and want to settle on the farm.

The next day, before I took off for the long trip back to Indiana, I took my mother and Nancy up for their first (very short) flight.

Soon after we lifted off, and before I could even pull back on the throttle and start climbing out, my mother said:

"Okay, Son, that was a fine ride. Let's land now."

Back in Ft. Wayne, a young lady named Kay Gehrig was working as a chemist in the lab that summer. A student at Goucher College in Baltimore, she knew Agnes and had attended our wedding. The two girls had been in high school together, where Kay had been editor of the school paper and salutatorian of her class.

I needed some extra help with statistical analysis and moved Kay from the chemistry lab into my small office. It was a rather dull job, plotting reams of data into frequency distribution curves. Kay did the job accurately with more output than anyone else. She sharpened the pencils frequently enough to make very fine lines, and her cross-hatched frequency distribution curves were quite attractive.

Kay was very bright — brilliant, in fact. One of her professors at Goucher said she was "my *cum laude* girl" and she would have been if she hadn't dropped out after her junior year. Kay also was attractive; physically striking, with long, dark-blonde hair and big eyes. She was well endowed.

I was distracted as she sat next to me, drawing curves. I'd lose my concentration, and I'm sure she knew it. This was Kay's second summer at the lab, first as a chemist, then as an X-ray technician and now as a technical assistant to me. She made 65 cents an hour and hadn't received a raise when she came back for her second summer. She spoke to me about that, and we gave her a 5-cent-per-hour raise.

"I forgot to tell you: Thanks for the nickel," Kay said to me while leaving work a few days later, obviously thinking the "raise" an insult.

I was ready to leave the office, too, and asked, "May I walk home with you?"

"Why not? I'm headed that way anyway."

Later, I took her for a ride in the Stinson, and she bubbled with enthusiasm about the opportunity to fly. During the next few weeks, I was with Kay all day and dated her at night. I sure was lonesome when she returned to school for her junior year.

During my second year at Ft. Wayne, there was a catastrophic failure of a supercharger turbine wheel on a B17 bomber. Luckily, the plane had limped home and landed safely.

A certain Major Sams called a meeting to investigate the failure, and I was present with other GE engineers. Major Sams turned out to be my old professor of mechanical engineering at Clemson! He had been called into the service, was in the Air Corps and had been assigned to Wright-Patterson Field in Ohio, the renowned Air Corps aviation laboratory during World War II.

It was seven years since Prof. Sams had inspired me with his technical lectures at Clemson. I was delighted to see him again, and we had a nostalgic talk about our Clemson days. He knew that Sir Frank Whittle was stationed at the GE supercharger plant at Lynn, Mass., and was working with GE engineers designing the first gas turbines for jet fighters. The intervening eight years and the technical challenges of the war had carried many of Prof. Sams's ideas into reality. The GE gas turbine-powered jet fighter planes entered combat in Europe the following year.

Another application for the turbo-supercharger will give you a better taste of wartime engineering and metallurgy. The turbo-supercharger on the famous and versatile P38 interceptor is mounted atop each of the dual booms that stretch from

The versatile P38.   -Hall of History, Schenectady, N.Y.

behind each engine to the dual tail surfaces, in line with the trailing edge of the wing. The supercharger's horizontal turbine wheels are located midway on the boom and are in direct line with the pilot's neck. The P38 had a ring mounted beside the turbine wheel to deflect it away from the line of the pilot's head in case it failed. The wheel runs red hot and rotates at 10,000 rpm, near the strength limit of the best known materials.

By this time, the GE Moss supercharger was standard equipment on the B17 "Flying Fortress," the B24 "Liberator," the P47 "Thunderbolt," the P38 and, later, the B29 "Superfortress." They all were flying higher, faster and farther than planes had ever flown before, but failures of both the supercharger wheels and the blades were too frequent.

Early in World War II, the material used for the supercharger blades was an alloy designated as S495. I don't know where the name came from, but it might have been the "495" concoction mixed up in the Allegheny Ludlum Steel Co. lab in Watervliet, New York, in trying to develop a better high-temperature material. S495 was a complex mixture of metals that was so reactive to oxidation that it couldn't be melted in the atmospheric electric furnaces of that time. It had to be vacuum melted. But since vacuum melting was not yet a commercial process, it was air melted anyway, and the result always was a very "dirty" material forged into blades that frequently failed. Supercharger wheels also suffered from similar "dirty" steel-mill processing. Rotating at 10,000 rpms, the wheels frequently cracked and the blades too often flew away.

In a fateful decision, I became determined to find a solution to this problem.

6

METALLURGY AND GAS TURBINES

On the leading edge of aviation technology

In 1945, a few months before the end of World War II, General Electric transferred me from Ft. Wayne, Indiana, back to Schenectady, New York. As for the Stinson, I bought out my partners' interest and became that little beauty's sole owner.

I flew my Stinson to Schenectady and, when I landed, my old friend Jack Adamson was standing there beside an army trainer he had recently purchased. I hadn't seen him since 1940 when we had gotten our private licenses together in Lynn, Massachusetts.

Jack was very proud of his rugged plane, built to take the stress of acrobatics. I asked him if he had ever "looped it," and he said he had tried a few times but had never gotten all the way around.

"Let's go up and I'll show you how to loop it," I led with my chin.

"You're on," Jack replied. And off we flew up the Mohawk River Valley. I wondered if my bravado had landed me in deep trouble: Looping an airplane was not child's play.

After I'd spent about half an hour doing stalls and power dives, I felt I could loop it. I gave it full power, put the nose down in a steep dive and, when we reached 170 mph, pulled back on the stick. Pretty soon we were climbing up through the vertical quadrant in a loop. In the second quadrant we were upside down, on top.

I kept the "G" forces tight by holding back on the control stick, but as we were about ready to complete the top quadrant and head down, we lost speed. Just before the plane stalled and went into an upside-down spin, I rolled it over and settled back into normal flight.

"You can loop it, eh?" Jack smiled.

"Let me try again!" I replied, determined.

This time, I held the nose down until we reached 180 mph, and I

The army trainer

yanked the stick back into my gut until the "G" forces made me lightheaded.

But we still stalled just before flying over the top.

Jack said, "I can loop it."

"It's your ship, take it away," I came back.

By watching what I'd done wrong, Jack suddenly was able to loop it as though he'd been circling over the top all his life. To this day, I'm still not sure what my problem was.

A few months after I returned to Schenectady, the war ended, and American industry began the massive transition from war materials back to civilian production. Automobiles, houses, washing machines, toasters and nylon stockings took the place of tanks, warplanes, shells and olive-drab material on American assembly lines. Panty hose hadn't been invented yet.

These were the years that Republic Aviation built the amphibious Seabee, which was supposed to put the seaplane into every fisherman's tackle box, but casting for trout while standing in the cabin never appealed to anyone.

The supercharger plant at Ft. Wayne closed quickly, and people were laid off by the hundreds. Engineers interviewed for jobs inside and outside GE. I wasn't nervous about my future because GE had approved a major expansion plan that included a new and bigger research lab. I'd been invited back to Schenectady to develop new, high-temperature alloys and new processes for producing them.

Before this, much of the development in this new field had been done during GE-sponsored work at special steel companies. A lot of the early work was guided by Bill Badger, the chief metallurgist at the supercharger plant in Lynn, Mass.

Steel companies then and now haven't been noted for their research acumen. Yet GE depended on improvements in high-temperature metals before it could develop efficient and dependable gas turbines for commercial aircraft. Typical of GE's technical excellence, the company organized a substantial expansion and backed it up with millions of dollars.

I had developed lots of ideas for high temperature alloy research. Along with dozens of Ph.D.s, in physics and chemistry, including Nobel laureate Irvin Langmuer, I undertook my new job as a research metallurgist at the great new GE research center on the banks of the Mohawk River.

At the beginning of the war, one of GE's few research metallurgists, Rudy Thielman, had found by serendipity that a nickel-cobalt-chromium alloy called "Vitallium," originally developed for dental and medical hardware applications, was superior to all the alloys then being used for supercharger blades. From this alloy, Thielman precision-cast blades by the lost-wax process and daringly welded them to the supercharger wheel. The method was adapted as the standard for the production of the later wartime turbo-superchargers.

Just before I arrived at the GE lab, Thielman took a job at Pratt and Whitney Aircraft Corp. in East Hartford, Connecticut, GE's competitor in gas-turbine manufacturing. A year after that, he invented another superior alloy for gas-turbine blades that he appropriately named "Waspalloy." The name came from the great series of wartime Pratt and Whitney radial internal-combustion engines called "Wasps."

Today, over 50 years later, Waspalloy still is being used in many critical turbine parts that operate at high temperatures. Over the years, Waspalloy has undergone many alterations, with different alloying elements added to the recipe. It wasn't enough to add a few percentages of half a dozen hardening elements to the solution of nickel, cobalt and chromium, but now pinches of boron and phos-

GE's Alan Howard and Dr. Chapman Walker work on the world's first turboprop, the GE TG-100, ca. 1945.

-Hall of History, Schenectady, N.Y.

phorus have been found to enhance Waspalloy's high-temperature strength.

Nobody really knows why such a strange multiple complex of metallic bedfellows make a superior high-temperature alloy. Some years ago, when I was a practicing metallurgist, I thought better properties came about with the discreet mixing of a wide variety of elements having different atomic sizes. They seem to heal the dislocations at grain boundaries, which are the weak link at high temperatures.

During the five years I was at the GE lab, I organized and managed a technical group of 15 doctors there. My claim to fame came from being involved in the development of vacuum melting, a special process for smelting that enhances the properties of all high-temperature alloys. This process became the standard for making super alloys.

Meanwhile, I spent all the time in the air that I could. One memorable flight in my Stinson was from Schenectady back to Ft. Wayne for a long weekend. It was in July and the temperature was 90 degrees, as hot and sultry as the weather ever gets in Schenectady. George White, a member of our co-op household, was from Cleveland and wanted to hitch a ride home with me. The two of us took off bright and early on a Saturday morning for our westward flight.

Before leaving Schenectady, we heard from a weather briefing that winds aloft were directly in our face all the way, blowing at 50 mph at 10,000 feet. That would make our trip tough sledding. The only good news they gave was that the winds aloft were greater at higher altitudes, so we should plan to fly low.

George and I took off, and I climbed to 2,000 feet to test the winds at that altitude. I set the course for the first leg of our flight at 265 degrees west. I could immediately see the smoke from the Niagara Mohawk power plant blowing horizontally in our direction. Our flight path followed the New York Central railroad tracks.

A half hour out of Schenectady, I knew we really did have a serious problem when a freight train headed for Buffalo passed below us. I made a quick calculation that we were traveling at only 50 mph.

I flew still lower, just above the treetops. It was almost too low: As we approached a hill that was well above the surrounding terrain and higher than I had estimated, I advanced the engine to full throttle, and with maximum power, we barely cleared the hill. I turned to George's ashen face, and quipped, "Weather man said, 'Fly low'."

George White is now the official architect of the United States Capitol. A few years ago, we had a reunion of that illustrious group of housemates we had called the "Wolves Den." George and his wife gave a lively dinner party for us at their lovely home in Georgetown. It was 50 years since we had lived together in Schenectady. I asked him if he remembered our flight from Schenectady to Cleveland.

"How could I ever forget it, Jim? The weatherman said, 'Fly low'," George responded without missing a beat.

On that flight, after leaving George in Cleveland, I reached Ft. Wayne after dark, and one of my former partners in the Stinson was waiting to meet me. When he heard the Stinson coming and saw my feeble landing light, he had the airport landing lights turned on. It's hard to imagine an airport of any size today that doesn't leave its landing lights on all night!

I had a delightful long weekend in Ft. Wayne. Kay Gehrig was spending the weekend there, too.

Shortly after I returned to Schenectady, I was anxious to make another trip in the Stinson. I flew to Baltimore, where I spent one night, and very early the next morning picked up Kay, who had just finished her junior year at Goucher College. We flew on to South Carolina so Kay could meet my mother.

Just after we took off from the small landing strip outside Baltimore and were climbing out over a river a few hundred feet from the end of the runway, the engine coughed and stopped. I was afraid I had more on my hands than just a simulated forced landing: a wet one. I followed the cardinal rules for this emergency: nose down, maintain flying speed, don't turn back. Fortunately, as is normal in flight, the propeller kept the engine rotating; something called "the wind-milling effect."

I unlatched the door and was ready to land in the river when the engine caught and we returned to normal speed. We limped barely above the treetops on the far side of the river bank and resumed the climb to cruising altitude. That unreliable engine had sputtered on me before, but never in such a critical situation. I had my fingers crossed for the rest of the flight and swore that if I ever got back to Schenectady in one piece I would get new rings, a valve job and new magnetos, or sell that bird.

We made it to South Carolina and I introduced Kay to my gregarious mother, who immediately developed a good rapport with her. Soon after we arrived, when Mother and I were alone, she surprised me (actually, she astonished me).

"Son, Kay certainly is a lovely girl, and she has a beautiful figure," Mother pronounced.

I had never before known my mother to notice that girls had figures.

We had a great week with Mother, and Kay and I had a delightful week with each other. We walked the Mill place, the Ivey place, the Johnson place and the home place, we talked and talked. It was a romantic time and I was thinking about marriage again.

We survived the tiring, 10-hour flight back to Ft. Wayne after getting badly lost once and luckily stumbling onto an airport. I dropped Kay off at her home there, and I was ready for the air again. Especially so when Kay's father asked her if she was not just in love with an airplane.

"He's not an Episcopalian, and besides that, the boy has been divorced," Kay's mother added.

E arly the next morning I was "wheels up" again for Schenectady. Headwinds were too strong for me to make it in one day, so I spent the night in Syracuse.

I took off the next morning before the fog lifted and found myself atop solid clouds. The Stinson's radio navigation system was imperfect at best, and I was worried about the hills just south of Schenectady. According to my elapsed time, estimated speed and unsure direction, I should have been over town. I let down through the clouds, and I prayed to Kay's Almighty Episcopal Fathers that the clouds would break before I hit the ground. Luckily, I descended into the clouds at 2,000 feet. I broke out at 1,000 feet, only a few hundred feet above the last 800-foot hills that adjoined the wide Hudson River valley to the south of my course, some 15 miles from Schenectady.

To avoid such embarrassment in the future, I determined to get an instrument rating.

B ecause Kay's parents objected to my being divorced, and we couldn't find an Episcopal priest willing to perform the ceremony, Kay and I were married by an assistant Methodist minister in Schenectady.

We bought a lot on Hilltop Road on the outskirts of Schenectady. Victor Civkin, a Russian architect who worked for the GE appliance division, designed our first house in modern style. The same architect designed four more houses for me in subsequent years as Kay and I moved from place to place with our growing household.

Things went very well for me at the GE lab. When I became adjunct professor at Rensselaer Polytechnic Institute, I taught a part-time course in high-temperature metallurgy to Ph.D. candidates. I should have called my good old friend John Borring and told him that now there was such a thing as a "high-temperature metallurgist".

Kay became a staunch and devout worker at St. George's Episcopal Church. Kay's good works were recognized in the community, and she was invited to join the Junior League. She served the League with time, energy and effectiveness as a volunteer for several worthwhile causes, first in Schenectady and later in the Pittsburgh chapter. These were happy times, and we formed many lasting friendships in Schenectady.

Within a year of the war's end, I heard again about the result of Sir Frank Whittle's stay at the Lynn, Mass., plant during the war. In

The first American jet fighter, with the GE I-40 engine, demonstrated at Schenectady in 1946. -Hall of History, Schenectady, N.Y.

collaboration with the engineers at Lynn, two Wittle/GE gas turbines were built, designated as I-16 and I-40, with thrust ratings of 1,600 and 4,000 pounds each.

The I-40 was installed in the first American jet fighter. Bill Ruder, my boss at the lab, and I were invited to attend a show at the Schenectady airport, where two jet fighters powered by the I-40 engine were demonstrated. The planes were not much bigger than my Stinson. They were all-aluminum, low-wing monoplanes with large forward air scoops on each side of the fuselage, designed to feed the gas turbine tons of air. There was a big opening in the tail where the hot gasses from the turbine were exhausted to propel the plane.

This was the first U.S. jet-powered fighter plane. Both planes flew in formation, stunting and diving low over the airport. The several hundred GE people invited to see the spectacle watched with pride as ones who'd had a hand in the development and application of gas turbines to jet propulsion.

The vacuum-melting process we developed at the research lab for producing exotic metals didn't exist in the special steel industry and certainly was ignored by big steel companies.

In the late '40s and early '50s, the case for vacuum melting high-temperature alloys was proven. Still the steel industry didn't stir. I frequently asked Guy Suits, vice president of GE research, to send me to a cornfield in Ohio, give me some working capital with a little "sweat equity," and I would make vacuum melting into a business.

Slowly, special steel companies such as Cyclops and Allegheny took a second and third look at the vacuum-melting process. I saw it as a new opportunity, finally, to move the technology into the special steel industry where it belonged.

In 1952, I was invited to speak at a British Iron and Steel Institute conference in London. This gave me a chance to visit Dr. Rohn, a pioneer in vacuum melting. He worked for Hareus Vacuumsmeltzer in Hamburg, West Germany.

I flew to Paris, my second commercial flight and my first flight overseas, on a Pan American Boeing Stratocruiser, a big ship. It carried 40 passengers, with sleeping accommodations for 10.

Needless to say, commercial air transportation had come a long way since my first commercial flight on a DC3 and this, my second, on a Boeing Stratocruiser,. Douglas had advanced from the taildragger DC3 to the larger, passenger-carrying DC4, with their first tricycle landing gear, to the pressurized DC6.

We took off from New York and, after a bountiful meal at which I consumed a whole bottle of wine, I climbed into the bunk above my seat and, with the drone of four noisy internal-combustion engines in my ear, quickly fell asleep.

We were supposed to fly non-stop to Paris, but the headwinds were too strong and we stopped for refueling in London. I woke up when we landed there about daybreak. We took off again, and after a sumptuous breakfast we descended through broken clouds to the sight of the Eiffel Tower. We circled, then landed at Orly field.

I took a train from Paris to Hamburg, and the visit with Dr. Rohn was an eye-opener. Wartime destruction still was evident everywhere. When he showed me masons laying the first bricks for reconstruction of his laboratory, Dr. Rohn said, with hardly any accent, "All of my vacuum-melting facilities were destroyed when this building was bombed."

Dr. Rohn and I were citizens of two countries that had just finished a war. Now we were as friendly as two scientists ever could be, interested in a new technology: vacuum melting.

The meetings in London were held in the Grand Civil Engineering Hall, and it was freezing cold. We wore pajamas under our clothes and carried blankets from our hotel rooms on the second day of the conference.

I enjoyed a generous helping of kippers for breakfast every morning, and a bath of steaming hot water thawed me out at night. I'm sure that my lectures in the Grand Civil Engineering Hall didn't thaw anybody out.

My private flying ended, for awhile, when I started building our first house in Schenectady. I could never have finished that house alone. My GE friend, Bill Oberly, appeared with a hammer, and Jack Adamson stopped by with a shovel to help. Kay and I moved in after our first son was born. I sold my Stinson and hung up flying.

My name had become fairly well known in the small world of metallurgy, and job offers from outside GE developed. After an interview with the vice president of technology at Allegheny Ludlum, I turned down that first outside offer. I had serious conversations about going into the metals business with an older gentleman from Cleveland.

Then a longtime metallurgy friend, Chuck Evans, invited me to Cyclops in Pittsburgh to discuss a new position with them as director of research and development. Our first meetings took place in the nice little downtown office building. The next day, Chuck took me to the Bridgeville Works, in the valley below town. As we approached the creek by the plant, we had to stop and wait for two tractor trailers to exit the mill; the only entrance to the plant was a one-way bridge. As we toured the mill, I noticed that it completely filled a banana-shaped area between a creek on one side and railroad tracks on the other.

Nevertheless, we agreed to set up Cyclops's first research lab and to install a pilot plant for vacuum melting high-temperature alloys. The great character of the Cyclops officers and their sincere appropriation of half a million dollars to start made me realize that maybe the time had arrived for at least this special steel company to become an innovator.

They also told me they were ready to plan for a new plant site that wouldn't flood every time it rained too hard. They flattered me

The Lockheed Constellation   -Courtesy Lockheed Martin Corp.

by saying they needed a "spark plug" to help them expand.

I accepted the position at Cyclops as director of research and development and moved to a new life in Pittsburgh. Leaving GE wasn't easy after 16 fruitful, satisfying and certainly educational years. I left four years before my equity in the GE pension fund was vested.

The president of Cyclops organized a four-man planning committee, and for our first meeting we flew non-stop from Pittsburgh to Miami in a four-engine, pressurized Lockheed Constellation at 300 mph. It was a plane so good-looking it even was pretty while sitting on the ground. This was a far more comfortable ride than my first experience in a DC3 because, supercharged and pressurized, it could fly at 20,000 feet.

On the flight down, we passed directly over Charlotte, North Carolina, not far from my old hometown, and I was impressed by the activity at the Charlotte airport. It had grown to a commercial metropolis in comparison with the old Charlotte airport where, in 1934, I had rented an Aeronca to take my brother John Ed for that flight down the South Carolina rivers to the sea.

I don't remember what planning we accomplished on that Miami trip, but I do remember that the only bonefish caught in three days of fishing in the Florida Keys was the 12 pounder I landed after a long tussle. I had it mounted, and it cluttered my office wall for years before Kay decided it was too moldy to keep.

For me, another first in commercial flying was on a trip from Pittsburgh to Washington, D.C., on Allegheny Airlines in their pioneering Viscount Turboprop, which cruised at 400 mph. This was a British plane powered by Rolls Royce gas turbines. It had conventional propellers, the first major step between internal-combustion engines and pure jets. The jets came a year later with the introduction of the Douglas DC7 and the Boeing 707. They flew at 500 mph.

The last year I was at Cyclops, I was the only full-time member of the long-range planning committee. The other members were three 73 year-old retired officers and two current officers. We persuaded the board to build a new, stainless-steel strip plant on 1,000 acres we had purchased for Cyclops between a four-lane highway and a large river near Coshocton, Ohio. I'll never forget the day we showed the new plant layout to the Cyclops Board of Directors.

Without the knowledge of Mr. Stockdale, our aristocratic retired chairman, and the other older members of the planning committee, I had sneaked in a 3,000-foot landing strip on the backside of the property, between the mill and the river. I pointed out that the driving time between Bridgeville and Coshocton was four hours, and the flying time in the future Cyclops plane I was lobbying for would be only 40 minutes. I had named the strip on the layout, "The Stockdale Landing Field." I was pleased to see that gentleman burst out laughing rather than put hands around my neck when he took in the full meaning of the map.

A few years later, after I'd started flying again, Bill Stewart, Cyclops CEO, invited me to fly my Baron up to Pittsburgh, where I met the pilot of — guess what? The new Cyclops plane! He flew me to Coshocton, where we landed on the Stockdale strip. I had a guided tour of the most modern stainless-strip mill in all the industrial world at that time.

After three years at Cyclops, when things were humming along and we were beginning to expand, problems arose. The cost of the aggressive push to maintain our recently acquired leadership in special metals was resisted, and eventually rejected, by the Cyclops management. They preferred money in the bank rather than risking it with aggressive innovations into other new metals that had to be vacuum melted; titanium, molybdenum, zirconium and columbium.

I concluded that a new company was necessary to lead the special metals industry in exotic metals. Thus, I left Cyclops and founded my own company: Allvac Metals.

7

FOUNDING
ALLVAC METALS

Flying for business and pleasure

I resigned from Cyclops and struck out on my own to prove that I could stand alone. It was 1957, and I wanted to prove I could create a new company based on vacuum melting of high-temperature metals. Before I even had financing for the new company, a plant site or any organization, I named my new dream "Allvac Metals." The name "Allvac" proclaimed my intention to "ALWAYS" melt under a vacuum and never to use old Pittsburgh air-melting methods that produced "dirty" alloys.

My itch to create a company didn't appear overnight. The idea sprouted when I worked in the GE research laboratory, after I saw the virtues of a new technology for producing special metals. The idea jelled when I was at Cyclops and I saw the new technology being reduced to practice, but ever so reluctantly, within the steel industry.

After resigning from Cyclops, I took a Northeast tour to forge shops and machine shops, and I picked up a smattering of orders even before I had a plant. I called on my old friend and old boss, Bill Badger, at the GE plant in Lynn, Massachusetts, where I had worked for two years. He not only refused to give me a trial order, but thought I was foolish to undertake the formidable, and in his opinion, impossible task of founding a new company.

At Pratt and Whitney Aircraft Corp. in East Hartford, Connecticut, the second largest manufacturer of jet engines, I visited the chief metallurgist and the purchasing agent. I pressed hard for an experimental order, but to no avail.

"The process of having new suppliers approved, you know, takes one or two years," they sniffed.

Pratt and Whitney had just opened a new jet-engine development plant in West Palm Beach, Florida, and I was advised to go there. I did, and came back with trial orders from them. Still, I was very discouraged because I thought metallurgy friends at GE and Pratt and Whitney surely would welcome me, the metallurgist in business, with a bundle of orders.

Often, one's greatest expectations are the least realizable. Here I was with a wife, four children, a high standard of living and no salary. All the money I had was committed to this new business venture. I couldn't waste time pondering my plight, but had to rush on and incorporate a company, have a public venture-capital offering, hire a few key people, order equipment and find a plant site.

While exploring for a Cyclops plant site the year before, I'd learned about the industrial advantages of North Carolina; it seemed an ideal state for a new venture. The availability and cost of power and gas were competitive with other eastern states. We were high-tech, and the melting and processing to be practiced by Allvac were new. It would be easier to train southern workers having a strong work ethic than to re-train experienced, unionized labor. North Carolina was well removed from the United Steel Workers and frowned on all labor unions.

Customers for our products were peppered through the Midwest, the Northeast and the West Coast, with only one in Florida. After Allvac became established, we would expect to supply material to Rolls Royce in England, the third largest producer of jet engines. So there was hardly a geographically central location for a plant. The cost per pound of high-temperature alloys was in the $5 range, so a few cents per pound extra shipping cost was not a big factor, but labor costs were a huge factor. Southern labor could start at $1 per hour, compared with $20 per-hour union labor in Pittsburgh and all the Midwestern states.

As I looked into financing along the Eastern Seaboard, I quickly focused again on North Carolina and soon settled Allvac in Monroe, a town of about 10,000 people with a small airport and only 25 miles from Charlotte, where there was a rapidly growing commercial airport. Local businessmen invested, some in Allvac Metals and others in the first Allvac building. We located the plant within the Monroe city limits, which recently had been extended to include what had been Camp Sutton during the war, a staging area for GIs bound for Europe.

66

Van Secrest, a prominent merchant and farmer, invested in both the new building and in Allvac stock, and he became a local director at Allvac. My brother Oliver joined me as a vice president. He became the most valuable officer and made lasting contributions to the success of my fledgling company. Hank Rowan, an old friend who operated his own induction-heating business, agreed to be a director. He also supplied induction-heating equipment for our vacuum-melting furnaces.

In 1957, when Rowan attended the first Allvac Metals board meeting, he flew down from Rancocas, New Jersey, in his recently acquired single-engine, two-passenger Aircoup. It took Hank eight hours to fly the Aircoup back to New Jersey, and he couldn't face the additional five hours it would have taken to fly on to his summer place at Lake George in upper New York state, where he was headed for the weekend. When he stopped for fuel at Middletown, N.J., he asked the airport manager if he had a faster plane. On the spot, he traded his Aircoup for a 150-mph Bellanca and continued his trip at a faster pace! This was the beginning of the habit Hank developed for frequently trading his old plane for a newer, faster and bigger one.

Hank Rowan and his son in Hank's Aircoup.

S oon after starting Allvac, I wanted to buy a large blooming mill to reduce the cost and time of sending our cast ingots to Pittsburgh for conversion to billets and bars. Atlantic Steel placed a suitable used blooming mill on the market.

By this time, Hank Rowan had upgraded his fleet again with a recently acquired Piper Twin Apache, and he offered to fly down and pick up three of our directors for a flight to Atlanta to inspect the blooming mill. The four of us climbed aboard Hank's Apache and took off for Atlanta. It was a rainy day in the Charlotte area, and I was a little nervous when the weather turned worse and Hank had to file an instrument flight plan. That was before I got my instrument rating, and I wasn't much help to him. He was pretty busy climbing out from Monroe and talking to Charlotte control. Fortunately, his Apache had an automatic pilot, and as soon as we had set our short course to Charlotte, he was able to flick it on. Then he could use both hands to change frequencies and handle the mike for an instrument flight rules (IFR) flight.

I looked in the back seat and saw two nervous older men with clenched fists and white knuckles. The flight took only an hour, and we landed at the Peachtree airport in Atlanta with a 1,000-foot ceiling. Olin Nisbet (a cousin) and Harry Dalton recovered fairly well during the taxi ride from the airport to Atlantic Steel.

There, the president and two other hospitable officers met us. They took us on a tour of the Atlantic Steel facilities and showed us the huge blooming mill. It was impressive, with a 12-foot-high, 300-hp electric-motor drive. After a pleasant lunch with the officers of Atlantic Steel, we were driven back to Peachtree and flew back to Monroe in much improved visual flight rules (VFR) weather.

At a meeting back home, I proposed to the directors that since we didn't have two dimes to rub together in the Allvac bank account, we form a new company and sell $100,000 worth of stock, then buy the mill for $80,000. The good thing about financially well off directors is that they can come to the rescue of a fledgling company when called upon.

Olin Nisbet, head of Interstates Securities in Charlotte, agreed to a new underwriting to finance the Southern Rolling Mills Co., based on the guarantee that all Allvac directors would subscribe to the new issue of stock. We bought the rolling mill and I turned to the task of moving it to Monroe.

S hortly after I organized Allvac, and Kay and I had settled the family in Monroe, I learned that Jack Adamson had transferred from Schenectady to Charlotte to take charge of GE's service shop there. Kay and I renewed our friendship with Jack and his saintly wife, Mary. At dinner with them a few weeks before, Jack had expressed an interest in joining Allvac to take charge of manufacturing. He'd been a foreman for several years at GE before moving to Charlotte, and I knew about his ability to get big jobs done despite, or perhaps because of, his abrasive personality.

I asked Jack if he'd like a challenge. My proposition was that he come to work at Allvac at his current GE salary. His first job would be to disassemble the Atlantic Steel rolling mill, move it to Monroe, build a new structure in Monroe to house it, and reinstall the mill there, all within three months. If accomplished, he would receive a $3,000 bonus and a job as vice president of manufacturing at Allvac. Jack said he would take the job under one condition.

"I'm not very interested in conditions," I told him.

But when he added, "I'll take the job and I can do it, but only if you buy an airplane so I can commute to Atlanta.

"We have a deal!" I answered.

This was a week before Christmas in 1960. It just happened that a dentist from Gastonia had been trying to sell me his Navion. I called him and was able to buy it for $8,500. I attached one request: The dentist had to deliver the plane to Monroe on Saturday and check out both Jack and I on flying it.

"I hope both of you have flown a retractable-gear plane," he said.

"Neither of us have," I replied.

"Well, I'm not sure I can accomplish that for both of you in one day."

"You'd better try real hard, because Jack has to fly the Navion to Atlanta early Sunday morning," I told him.

Jack, the Monroe airport manager, the dentist and I all climbed aboard and spent six hours flying together with either Jack or I at the controls, doing touch-and-go landings. Finally, we both soloed and added a retractable-gear plane rating to our private pilot licenses.

F rom the retractable-gear Navion through the retractable-gear Barons that I subsequently owned, I got in a habit of saying "wheels up" as soon as I flicked the switch to raise the landing gear. So "wheels up" was added to our family vocabulary, and it became the standard reference for announcing our departure times for flying. Naturally, the only title I ever thought about for this book was *Wheels Up*.

Of course the term has a double meaning: Wheels are up when the plane leaves the ground and up again, if it has retractable land-

The Navion

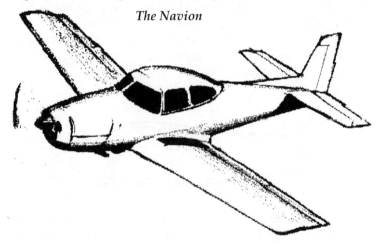

ing gear, when they are retracted and hidden away in the wing and fuselage, but we won't confuse things by worrying about that.

Jack took off Sunday morning for Atlanta in the all-aluminum, low-wing, four-passenger Navion with two maintenance men from Allvac. They started to disassemble the blooming mill on Christmas Eve, when it was 28 degrees. On April 1, three months later, after 15 round trips in the Navion between Monroe and Atlanta, and after four wide-load truckloads from Atlanta to Monroe, our new bloomer was installed. It rolled the first ingots in a new building on the Allvac campus, next door to the recently installed, 10,000-pound induction-vacuum melting furnace, the largest in the world.

Not much grass grew under our feet during the formative years at Allvac!

After this, we put the Navion to good use flying our salesmen to faraway places and freighting special orders to customers who were willing to pay the extra cost for special delivery of experimental alloys.

To maximize the advantages of business flying, we often found it necessary to fly at night and in bad weather. This raised the question about upgrading to a twin-engine plane better equipped for blind flying. When a used, low time, 260-hp, four-passenger twin Beechcraft Baron was put on the market by Burlington Mills in Greensboro, N.C., I decided to buy the larger and faster plane.

A few months before this development, a dapper, instrument-rated retired Air Force pilot named Jim Russell appeared at the Monroe airport, and I hired him to be our pilot. He and I flew to the Greensboro airport. I will always remember my feelings of surprise and pleasure when I first saw the neat little twin Baron 55 sitting in the Burlington hanger.

The Baron 55

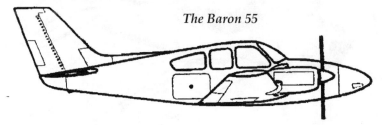

I knew we had to have this new working toy. It was well equipped for blind flying, and it had one of the best instruments ever designed for the private pilot: an automatic pilot. I bought the Baron for $38,000. Jim Russell flew it back to Monroe that day while I returned with the Navion.

I got checked out in the twin Baron and added the "multi-engine" rating to my private license. After we sold the Navion, Jack bought a Cessna 190 and flew it a great deal on Allvac business. It was a closed-cabin four-seater with a big Wright 250-hp radial engine, and it was a taildragger.

The Cessna 190

A few years later, in a feeling typical of boat owners and flyers, I wanted more horsepower for more speed and better instrumentation. I replaced my first 520-hp Baron that cruised at 210 mph with another that had two 285-hp engines, for a total of 570 hp. It cruised at 230 mph. The new plane also had better NavCom dual radios and deicing boots on the wings and tail. It had a new DME, a distance-measuring device, a very useful instrument that continuously records the distances and ground speeds to VOR radio stations.

This plane cost me $101,000. I understand that a new, well equipped Baron today, in 1997, costs $500,000.

The Baron 55B   -*Collection of the author*

Just after I bought the new Baron, Hank Rowan flew down from New Jersey for an Allvac directors meeting in his fifth plane, a supercharged Cessna 320 Skyknight. Sometime before this meeting I had claimed that my new Baron was faster than his old Cessna 310, and I had challenged him to a race. Both the Baron and the Cessna 310 had the same 285-hp engines.

When he bought the new, faster, supercharged Cessna 320, he was ready to race. I still bet with him that my Baron was faster than his plane, up to an altitude of 10,000 feet. Above that, his supercharger would, of course, provide more horsepower, and certainly the 320 would be faster.

After the directors meeting, on a sunny summer afternoon, we decided to race from Monroe to Philadelphia. We took off from the old Monroe airport with prearranged, standard engine settings, and we kept in touch by radio, giving each other periodic DME readings showing the distance to the next Omni radio station, and ground speeds.

At 8,000 feet, over Richmond, I was 10 miles ahead. But between 8,000 and 10,000 feet, his superchargers took over, so Hank caught up and passed me before we reached the Delaware Memorial Bridge. I was 10 miles behind when he landed at his strip, behind his 1,000-acre industrial campus in Rancocas, N.J. I landed a few minutes later.

The Cessna 320

I spent the night with Hank and his wife, Betty, at their home in Rancocas. Early the next morning, at Hank's strip, I fired up my Baron, ready to continue my trip to Hartford, Conn. After checking out the engines and feathering the props, I gave her full throttle and headed down the runway with an eye out for the power line at the opposite end. As I approached take-off speed, and just before I was ready to pull back on the wheel for lift-off, the left engine coughed and stopped dead. I immediately cut the right engine, and I braked the plane to a stop just a few hundred feet short of the 23,000-volt power line at the end of the runway.

It didn't take long to diagnose the problem. My fuel management had gone awry, and I was trying to take off on empty auxiliary fuel tanks! My habit of switching the fuel tanks from mains to "auxs" soon after taking off, leaving them there until one engine coughed empty before switching back to the main tanks, had almost done me in. In the excitement of our race, I had failed to exercise the standard procedure of never landing on the auxiliary tanks and had failed to switch the engines back to the main tanks the night before when I landed. I also failed the basic fuel-management procedure by not checking to see that the fuel was on the main tanks before taking off that morning.

If the engine had coughed 10 seconds later, I would have been in the most critical posture of a twin-engine flight, just after lift-off, just above stalling speed, before cleaning up the plane by raising the flaps and landing gear. When confronted with this situation, the inviolate rule is: Don't dare try to turn back, but get the nose down, keep on straight ahead, hope the power line can be cleared and that there is plenty of hay in the diary barn beyond to cushion a crash.

My brother Oliver and his wife, Ida, didn't share my enthusiasm for flying. Usually, he would find some excuse to go by commercial airliner rather than fly in the Baron, especially if I was going on the trip and we weren't taking our professional pilot. I even offered to build a landing strip on his farm and suggested that with that, he could be picked up there at 7 a.m. and be at the GE Evendale gas turbine for a meeting at 9. On the same day, he would have time to fly on to Akron for another two-hour meeting with our favorite forge-shop customer, then be back home for dinner at 7 p.m.

Eventually, I found out, a least partly, why Oliver wasn't enthusiastic about flying with me in a small plane. I'd flown up to Muskegan, Michigan, to meet Oliver for a sales call. He'd been traveling all week, and I knew that after the meeting in Muskegan he wouldn't want to drive to Detroit to catch a late flight back to Charlotte.

"Oliver, why don't you climb in the Baron with me, and we'll be home for dinner," I said.

He surprised me by saying, "Okay, I'll join you under one condition: That you don't tell Ida."

8

KAY LEARNS TO FLY

Building Aero Plantation

In 1962, our two daughters, Mary and Holly, were enrolled in
the Country Day School in Charlotte, North Carolina, and Kay
and I talked seriously about moving half-way between Charlotte and Monroe, N.C., to shorten the 25-mile commute. We also
knew that the old Monroe airport soon would close and that the
city showed no inclination to build a new one. I knew we couldn't
easily give up our Allvac Metals Co. plane because our customers
were scattered far and wide. Nor could Kay and I easily set aside
our own passion for flying.

I already had replaced my first Baron with a faster, better-
equipped model. I knew that business flying would be an indis-
pensable link for our growing company even though Charley
Truesdell, our treasurer, thought of flying as an unnecessary and
extravagant business expense. But when I coupled our school transportation problem with our personal interest in flying, adding my
company's need for business flying, I knew all three problems could
be solved by buying a large tract between Monroe and Charlotte,
and building a new house and landing strip there.

I called on an old farm Realtor, Mr. Howe, who knew the owner
of every acre in Union County, and told him what I needed. In a
few weeks, he came up with 250 acres that were for sale near the
village of Weddington, midway between Charlotte and Monroe, and
an option on two adjoining tracts, for a total potential spread of 500
acres. Having been raised on a large farm in South Carolina, I
thought 500 acres should be the minimum for a suitable country
estate. It was big enough for a private landing strip, large lakes and
a few extravagances. Of course, I wanted a herd of cows. The price
was right, averaging $250 an acre for the first tract.

After walking the property several times and deciding that I could
clear a half-mile by 500-foot wide area for a landing strip that faced
the prevailing northeast wind, I told the Realtor to consummate the

deal for the entire tract, and we named it Aero Plantation.

I spent the next several weekends walking every acre of the land over and over again until I had the terrain fixed in my mind. I hired a bulldozer operator and told him to follow me and clear a path the width of his blade. I started in the southwest corner of the property, holding a compass, and I walked 50 degrees northeast, in the direction of the prevailing winds. The walk ended at 2,500 feet, after I reached the creek that ran through the middle of the property. The line cut by the bulldozer's blade became the centerline of the landing strip.

I remember the exact date of that eventful walk because later that day a friend came by to tell me the startling news that President John F. Kennedy had been shot. It was Nov. 22, 1963.

The strip area was about half pasture and half woods. In a couple of weeks, the bulldozer man cleared and leveled the terrain. He also cut a half-mile road from the creek end of the strip to the highway between Weddington and Monroe, 12 miles from Allvac Metals in Monroe and 12 miles from Country Day in Charlotte. He also cleared a site and dug a foundation for my new house. Naturally, it would be located atop the highest hill on the property, a convenient distance to taxi a plane.

After the grading was finished I could hardly wait to drive over to the old Monroe airport to fire up my Baron and fly it back for the first landing at Aero Plantation. Nearby neighbors gathered to see if the plane they saw descending into the woods had crashed, and they were surprised to see my Baron parked at the end of a fresh, red-clay landing strip.

To minimize the amount of grading necessary to level the strip, it was left on a slight incline, about 20 feet higher on the northwest end. This had the effect of lengthening the strip by the equivalent of several hundred feet when landing uphill and taking off downhill. These landing and take-off directions could be used almost without exception because the wind was hardly ever blowing at more than 10 knots, the break-point in deciding to land by wind direction instead of by the grade.

I invited Dr. Leslie Macleod, who owned the farm next door, to fly with me back to Monroe, where I would leave the Baron until the strip was paved. On the way out I christened the new landing strip with a little show for the crowd. I set the flaps at 20 degrees to maximize lift, I set the throttles, the mixture and the props wide open, and I held the plane still with the brakes, waiting until the two engines roared to full power. When I released the brakes, the Baron leaped forward like a race horse jumping out of the gate. We sped down the dirt strip, bathing the crowd in a cloud of red dust. I held her on the ground until the airspeed indicator hit 85 mph, 15 mph above minimum lift-off speed, I rotated and pointed the nose skyward in a steep, 3,000 foot-per-minute climb.

By the time we passed over the building site for my new house, we were 1,500 feet in the air. And when we passed over Leslie's adjoining farm, we were at 2,000 feet. I'm sure his wife, Jonnie, couldn't see us waving as we flew over.

The crowd on the ground was dumbfounded as they wiped dust from their eyes. The older people remembered having picked cotton in that very pasture not too many years before.

I called Victor Civkin, the GE household appliance architect who had designed the first house I built in Schenectady, a second house in Pittsburgh and a third house in Monroe. I asked him to build a fourth, six-bedroom house — with a plane port — at Aero Plantation.

While the house design was being completed, the bulldozer operator built a dam near the end of the landing strip to impound water for a 25-acre lake, the first of a dozen lakes I eventually built on the property. The bulldozer's stay at Aero Plantation lasted a lot longer than originally planned. More lakes and a nine-hole golf course were added to the earth mover's plate, and he moved thousands of yards of dirt before he finished.

Soon after completing the grading, paving and lighting for the landing strip, I applied to the FAA for an official instrument-landing approach off the Fort Mill VOR (a ground-based electronic navigation system) 10 miles due west of Aero.

Remember Fort Mill? It was Colonel Elliot Springs's hometown and the place where he built a landing strip next to his father's house in the 1920s. To me, however, the FAA sniffed that I had an illegal landing strip because I hadn't asked for their approval before building it. I didn't pursue the matter, but for the next 25 years I made unofficial VOR instrument approaches into Aero.

Over a period of 25 years, I flew out of Aero Plantation a few thousand times. There were only three occasions when I couldn't land there because of bad weather.

The author's home -- complete with plane port -- at Aero Plantation

Kay had been enthusiastic about flying since I'd courted her by plane in 1945. In 1962, after our four children were in school and Allvac Metals was prospering, Kay had begun flying lessons at the old airport near our Monroe home.

Her first instructor was Jim Russell, the dashing young pilot who flew our Allvac Navion and Barons. Jim had an attractive personal manner, and he quickly became the most popular instructor at the airport. Just as quickly, he got in trouble with John Gulledge, the Monroe airport manager, because Jim had no official status and was taking work away from Gulledge and Pete Poteet, an earlier manager and then instructor.

When Pete was airport manager, he'd slept in a room in the back of the hangar with a .45 pistol nearby. People scratched their heads about where he'd come from and why, and what he might be up to. Late one night, someone rumored to be the disgruntled husband of a girl who had been too friendly with Pete, broke into the hangar and into Pete's room, ready for a fight to the finish. Pete wasn't there. As the invader was searching for him under the bed, he heard a plane start up outside the hangar. He rushed out and gave chase, but all he could do was fire three shots as Pete lifted off and flew away.

The next day, an airport pilot discovered curtains above the headboard of Pete's bed and, behind them, a door to the outside. Pete had long ago prepared for an unfriendly intruder. He had easily slipped away and disappeared!

After 10 hours of instruction from Jim Russell in a new-model Taylorcraft trainer I'd rented, Kay soloed and started building up flight time, working toward the 35-hour minimum required for her private license. This Taylorcraft had tandem seats, tricycle landing gear and was powered by a 50-hp engine.

Once I took Kay for a ride, flying the Taylorcraft from the back seat. When Kay climbed out first, from the front seat ahead of me, the center of gravity shifted behind the two rear wheels, too far back toward my abundance, so the nose wheel popped up off the ground and the tail sank. It looked like the earlier-model Taylorcraft taildragger!

Jim Russell got a franchise to sell a single-engine plane called a Maul. He sold one to a bootlegger in the North Carolina mountains, and I agreed to fly Jim to Michigan to pick it up. Kay went with us and got in a long cross-country flight by flying the Maul back to Monroe with Jim while I returned alone in the Baron.

When Jim delivered the plane to the bootlegger, he was paid in cash. Jim Russell had no problem handling delicate matters in those days before the IRS made it tougher to do so: like depositing $10,000 in cash!

Jim frequently flew the Navion to pick up our sons, Jim and Jack, when they were in boarding school in Kent, Connecticut. Kay usually went along and got in a lot of hours and instrument experience flying cross-country in a retractable-gear plane. I remember two trips that proved beyond a doubt that nothing phased Jim Russell.

One was in very bad weather near New York City. Rather than fly on to the smaller airport in Danbury, Conn., where we usually landed, he altered his instrument flight plan and landed at John F. Kennedy International Airport in the single-engine Navion. He learned his lesson when they made him taxi for what seemed like 10 miles to a parking place, charged him $35, and made him taxi a seeming 12 miles before clearing him to take off the next day.

On another occasion, when Jim returned alone late one night to bad weather around Monroe, he thought he would find out what kind of reception he might get at Fort Bragg, the Army air base in Fayetteville. They took him in for the night, but he had to see the commanding general and have the riot act read to him before they gave him permission to fly out the next morning. He never again landed there, but he was the kind of guy who might have, just for the hell of it, to see if the general remembered him!

Jim was always in trouble with his wife. One night he returned home very late after a long trip for Allvac when the Mrs. greeted him at the door with a glass of beer in his face. Then she pitched him a laundry bag filled with his clothes. He returned to the airport and slept in his car.

A fter Kay passed the written and flight exams and got her private license, I gave her a Cessna 150, the plane that had taken the Piper Cub's place as the most popular trainer. The 150 is a neat, single-engine two-seater, a high-wing monoplane with a starter and flaps. It cruises at about 140 mph and lands at 40 mph. It is, as pilots say, a very forgiving airplane. I landed it one time on a 600-foot-long dirt dam.

Kay's Cessna 150

Kay enjoyed climbing into her 150 with various friends and flying to Myrtle Beach, South Carolina, for a picnic. She also liked flying solo to Washington, D.C., for lunch with an old Goucher College roommate. We frequently flew together to Sunday "fly-ins" at different airports in the Carolinas, and we got to know other pilots in the area.

Only once did I get nervous about Kay's flying. She was taking night-flying instruction and was practicing touch-and-go landings at the Aero Plantation strip behind our house. A little different technique is necessary to land there. When landing uphill, the ground comes up to meet you faster than when landing at a perfectly flat airport. This causes you to hit the ground sooner than expected, and you might bounce a few times before settling in. In landing downhill, the effect is even worse, because as you pull up the nose and flare out to land, the ground is falling away below you faster than normal. If you're not on your toes, you'll stall too high and drop in, sometimes like a rock.

Because of the slope and the relatively feeble landing lights, night landing demands good depth perception, too. Kay's eyesight was weaker than average, and I think this caused her some difficulty with night landings. I watched her practice enough there to see that her flare-out was a bit ragged. I understood why she always planned for daylight arrivals whenever she could. But when it came to flying on instruments, I was the ragged one and Kay was as smooth as silk.

Kay liked the challenge of flying and always worked and studied for higher ratings. She advanced from a private pilot's license to a commercial license, and then went to work for the top tier, an airline transport rating.

During this time, we both were trying to get our instrument ratings by attending a night school in Charlotte. There was always a good reason not to show up, and it was easy to fall asleep when we did. Finally, we gave up on that, took a week off and flew down to a flight school in Ft. Worth, Texas. After a week of concentrated class work and flying, we both got our instrument ratings. Kay got a near-perfect score on the written part of the instrument exam, and I passed.

We found out that our instructor at Ft. Worth, D.G. Bartworth (we called him Bart), was looking for a more secure place as an instrument instructor. We brought him back to Charlotte and introduced him to Lindsay Hess, manager of the Rock Hill, S.C., airport, who was looking for a full-time instrument instructor. They clicked, at least for a while, and Bart set up shop with Lindsay at Rock Hill.

One time after both Kay and I got our instrument ratings, she picked me up in Winston-Salem, N.C., where I left the Baron for a 100-hour checkup. The weather was so bad that both of us had to make instrument approaches when we landed there. This was one of the very few times that bad weather kept us from landing at Aero Plantation, and we had to file an instrument flight plan for the trip back to Charlotte. Kay did all the flying, and I was her passenger in her Cessna 150.

I was really impressed by how well she kept the instrument landing system (ILS), localizer and glide-slope needles crossed and how accurately she broke out under a 300-foot ceiling directly in line with the threshold of the runway.

Later that day, Kay and I were loafing in the control tower waiting for our ride. About mid-afternoon, when the controllers changed shifts, one of the new ones started looking around the field.

"Did that little Cessna 150 land in this terrible weather?" he asked.

"Yes, it did," said the controller who was going off duty. "Kay

Nisbet, sitting right here talking to us, was flying it with Jim as her passenger. She flew it down the middle of the ILS slot half an hour ago and broke out under the fog smack in line with the runway, like she was flying for Eastern Airlines."

Loafing in the airport tower at Charlotte reminds me again of how much things have changed. Today, because of security problems, it's hard to get permission to even visit the control tower at any airport, much less loaf there. Yet, in earlier days, we knew the controllers at Charlotte and thought nothing of paying them a visit from time to time to thank them for taking care of us when we needed to find Aero Plantation on gloomy, rainy days.

The Atlanta airport took off with explosive growth a few years before Charlotte's did, and I well remember landing at Atlanta a few weeks after I got my instrument rating. Parallel runways had been opened only a few years before, and I was gliding down on the ILS on runway 15L—150-degree direction, left runway.

Just before breaking out of the clouds, the control tower called me, and I responded, "Baron 77 Alpha Papa."

"You are coming in on a parallel runway and veering too close to 15R," the controller warned.

He got my attention fast, and I sharpened up. When I broke out of the clouds at about 900 feet, I looked to my right and, sure enough, there was a Delta commercial flight doodling down beside me only a few hundred yards away!

After landing, I taxied in to the Butler general aviation Hangar #1. As I climbed out, the line boy, as was Butler's custom, placed a yard-square red carpet for me to step out on. In a nice Southern drawl he said, "Welcome to Atlanta."

I gave my standard instructions: "Top all four tanks and check oil to full on both engines, use non-detergent, and park it for an overnight stay."

While this was happening, I noticed a Gulfstream corporate jet taxiing out to runway 15L. The 15L runway was not very far away from Hanger #1. Soon the jet engines were revved up to full throttle, with the usual terribly loud blast. The plane just inched forward, gained speed and then rapidly accelerated down the runway. The pilot "rotated" the plane, and it lifted off with the jet engine's loudest scream.

The line boy looked at me and said, "That's the Coca Cola plane, and I always wondered how many cases of Coke they have to sell to get it off the ground."

"I have no idea, but I guess it might take all that McDonald's sells in Atlanta today and tomorrow," I quipped.

I crossed off the Atlanta airport, not only for instrument flying but also for VFR flying. Airports with parallel runways are for commercial pilots, not for instrument-rated private pilots. Staying clear of airline pilots reminded me of an encounter I once had with one.

"You and your copilot must get awfully bored sitting up there with nothing to do except when you land and take off," I said to him, not quite able to remove my tongue from my cheek.

The captain quietly said, "We stay busy — constantly watching out for private pilots."

In 1965, after we had criss-crossed the United States several times, Kay and I decided to take on the adventure of a lifetime: to fly the Baron to Europe! We bought all the necessary charts and maps, and we found out about fuel availability in England and on the continent. We plotted our course over the North Atlantic, with fuel stops in Boston, Newfoundland, Iceland, London, Paris, Rome and West Berlin.

This was before Kay was rated to fly a twin-engine plane, so she had to be checked out in the Baron and have her private certificate upgraded so she could be the official Baron co-pilot on the overseas

Charlotte to Paris
Across the North Atlantic

-Linda Winecoff

flight.

We called on Bart in Rock Hill and he gave Kay several hours of instruction. Kay was doing well and was about ready to solo. She and Bart were flying at the Gastonia airport, doing touch-and-go landings.

"One more landing and I'll get out. You're ready to solo," said Bart.

On the next round, with Bart still sitting in the right seat, they both forgot to lower the landing gear and skidded in on the belly! Bart called me at my office in Charlotte. He knew I'd be concerned as soon as I heard his voice, knowing he was checking Kay out in the Baron.

"Hello. Everything is all right, Jim," he was quick to say.

"Then why are you calling?" I replied just as quickly.

I could hardly believe his straightforward description of the accident. They were coming in for a fourth and final touch-and-go before he let Kay take the Baron on her solo flight. Both were preoccupied with the solo flight and both forgot to lower the landing gear!

During the three months we waited to get the Baron fixed, our enthusiasm for the European trip waned. I've been sorry ever since that we missed that daring adventure.

For a long time, Kay and I had been fascinated by the annual display of gliders flying over Aero Plantation in competition for the longest round-trip flights out of Chester, S.C., 25 miles away. Frequently, they couldn't make it back to their Chester base and would land at Aero Plantation. The only sight prettier than a glider, silently drifting in and landing at Aero, is one glider after another si-lently drifting in and land-ing, touching down on one half-hidden tire riding on a wheel up in

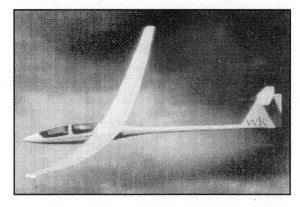

Jayne Reid's glider

the fuselage. They would roll off the pavement onto the grass, finally stopping as a wing lost its lift and settled to the ground.

The pilots' faithful crew chiefs, waiting at Chester airport, would be called and would arrive half an hour later in pickup trucks, pulling long, box-shaped trailers. The pilots would disassemble the gliders, tuck them away in the big boxes and drive off, only to come back the following year from far-away places like Brazil, California and Europe. Then they'd try once again to make it back to Chester without the stop-off that always thrilled the residents of Aero Plantation.

On the very next weekend after the accident at Gastonia, to temper our disappointment about the European trip, Kay and I flew down to the gliding school in Chester. We got checked out, soloed and added a glider rating to our pilot licenses! I believe that soaring in a glider, without the noise of an engine, might be the ultimate in flying experiences.

9

AERO PLANTATION

"His and Hers"

I n 1965, a few years after Kay and I moved our family to Aero Plantation, it was announced that the old Monroe airport would be closed and a shopping center built on the property. My old friend and Allvac Metals colleague Jack Adamson and a dozen others had their planes parked there. Jack asked me to sell him a couple of acres at Aero Plantation for a new house and a place to park his plane. I was reluctant at first, but I finally did sell Jack two acres, and he built the second house at Aero. But he refused to add a plane port to his residence!

I parked my Baron in the combination car and plane port built onto my house. That idea was too novel for Jack and his wife, Mary, so he parked his Cessna 190 at the end of the strip in the rain. He soon upgraded to the faster, retractable-gear 210.

The Cessna 210   -Courtesy Cessna Aircraft Corp., Div. of Textron

It wasn't long before Pete Larson, another flyer, came along and wanted to buy land at Aero. I traded him 25 acres for $15,000 and a Cessna 182. A few years later, Pete married a vivacious Swedish lady named Margaretta, and they built a fine house on the large lake above the landing strip and lived at Aero for 10 years. Pete parked his Cessna 310 in the yard of his new home.

The Cessna 310   -Courtesy Cessna Aircraft Corp., Div. of Textron

Then, Kathy "Big Cat" Davis, a private pilot and a retired airline stewardess, appeared and wanted to buy a lot. I certainly hadn't planned for Aero to be a residential development. But with the enthusiasm shown by Jack, Pete, Kathy and others to live and park their planes there, I changed my mind about keeping Aero as my private domain and decided that some of the cost of this capital sinkhole could be defrayed by selling off large lots.

"Big Cat" and her husband, Bud Davis, built a fine home with a plane port. Kathy flew in the Ninety-Niners (a ladies' flying organization) with Kay, and Bud flew from Aero on business for many years. He started with a Piper Arrow. As his business improved, he bought a Beech Bonanza, shown above parked in his home plane port. As his business continued to grow, he bought a Beechcraft Baron and finally a Duke. Fortunately, Bud never had an engine cough during the five years he flew the heavy, pressurized Duke off the short Aero strip.

So I subdivided the place into 107 large lots and set aside 100 acres for community property, which included the golf course, the landing strip and seven miles of private roads. Before my continuous building program was over, the community property

The Davis home at Aero Plantation.   -Kathy Davis

included a dozen lakes. Later, "The Places of Acres" was further identified by a unique sculpture designed by Tom Nun, an art professor at UNCC in Charlotte. People started calling his sculpture "The Thing."

An artist's rendering of the Aero Plantation sculpture we called "The Thing," by UNCC art professor Tom Nun.   -Collection of the Author

In 1968, Tom and Hansie Roboz from Tennessee came along and bought my original house. When I met the lovely Hansie Roboz she introduced me to her six year-old, identical twin daughters. When the two girls curtsied, I felt like a blue-blooded Duke. That is, until I met her husband, Tom Roboz, a pleasant, no-nonsense Hungarian. Tom introduced me to his two Berlin-trained German Shepherds, and they looked up and growled. Then he introduced me to his live-in German houseman, and he growled, too.

Tom wasn't a pilot but he was a visionary fellow, and he could see the advantage of being picked up at Aero and flying to his scattered plants in Tennessee and Georgia. He advanced from leasing Cessnas to a Piper Turboprop Cheyenne. It was powerful enough to routinely get off the short Aero strip and pass over my house at 2,000 feet. Jim Duncan, his pilot, also could pop it on the ground at the threshold of the runway, and by reversing the props, he could stop it in 1,200 feet, about half-way up the runway. I rode in the Cheyenne on several occasions and envied its high performance, far better than my Baron's.

Tom Roboz's Piper Cheyenne

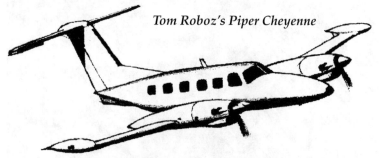

When Tom made his final offer for the first house I'd built at Aero, he added one request: "Move that hanger beside the house where your "His and Hers" airplanes are parked."

By this time, Kay had bought a twin Comanche, and we had built a hanger to park it and my Baron next to the house. I agreed to Tom's demand and moved the hangar to the end of the landing strip, where Kay and I parked our planes while I built my second, larger house on another hill overlooking the strip.

Later on, Hansie got the flying bug, quickly soloed, and continued flying instruction all the way to a private license and an instrument rating. I encouraged Hansie to fly. Tom always seemed a little nervous about it, and eventually she hung it up after becoming the third licensed aviatrix at Aero Plantation.

A fourth instrument-rated, licensed aviatrix, Holly Metzerott, an anesthesiology nurse, brought along her anesthesiologist husband, Dr. Kirk Metzerott. They became two of the most active flyers in the community. Kirk had flown for the Navy and enjoyed watching old movies with Navy planes landing on, and sometimes missing, the short flight decks of aircraft carriers. Today, he's half retired from his medical practice in favor of teaching all the sons and daughters of his medical friends to fly.

The Metzerotts' supercharged Piper

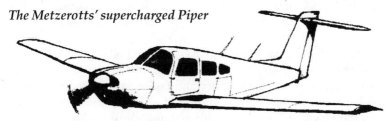

Holly once picked me up in Westerly, Rhode Island, in the Metzerotts' supercharged Piper and flew me back to North Carolina. I remember the trip very well because it was the first ride I had in a plane equipped with Loran navigation instrumentation. Under Holly's skillful use of it, she guided us into Aero as if we'd had Colonel Elliot Springs's OMNI navigation station sitting at the end of our strip.

A fter Christmas in 1965, I'd planned to fly my two boys back to school in Connecticut when I discovered the heater in the Baron was on the fritz. The boys were due back the following day, and by the time I found out that I couldn't get the heater fixed for a week or so because of the holidays, it was already late in the afternoon. We decided to have an early dinner, stock the plane with plenty of blankets and fly to Danbury without a heater.

It was a cold winter day. Now a cold day in Charlotte means below freezing, maybe as low as 20 during the night, and, of course, a lot colder if we traveled north at a high altitude. The normal temperature lapse rate with increasing altitude is three-and-one-half degrees per 1,000 feet. This translates to a temperature of 5 below zero outside the cabin at 10,000 feet. If the ground temperature over

Connecticut fell to zero by the time we got there in three hours, we could expect the outside temperature at 10,000 feet to be 35 below! Without heat, this could be called cold even in Siberia.

After the boys enjoyed a hearty dinner and we had loaded the Baron with our luggage and several blankets, darkness was falling at Aero Plantation. We climbed aboard and settled in with blankets around our shoulders, laps and feet. I fired up the engines and taxied to the southwestern end of the strip to take off downhill. As I flicked on the runway lights, a full moon peered over the treetops on the eastern horizon. I set the radio frequencies for the Greensboro radio, set the magnetic compass in the direction of the runway, checked to see that both fuel tanks were on mains, revved up each engine separately, checked the magnetos and feather-tested the props.

I looked in the back seat and asked, "Seat belts fastened?"

I revved up the engines to full throttle, full rich mixture and full prop pitch. Off we rolled, faster and faster, to 90 miles per hour. I pulled back on the controls and lifted off, retracted the gear, and throttled back to 2,500 rpm, with manifold pressure back to 25".

Aero Plantation was deep in the country and there were not many yard lights on the ground, but the glow from the city of Charlotte quickly appeared. The moon rose higher on the horizon, and the cabin was cold.

"ETA for Danbury, two hours and 50 minutes if we are not ice cakes before then," I announced cheerily.

We climbed to 10,500 feet. We were on a VFR flight plan, the skies were clear, and the moon lighted our cabin. We adjusted the blankets around our feet, our laps and our shoulders, and we were surprisingly comfortable even though the temperature outside was soon below zero.

Should we fly on to Danbury and land 20 miles from Kent, or should we put in at Newark, New Jersey, leave the Baron there for the heater to be repaired, and rent a car for a drive up to Kent?

We decided to put in at Newark, two hours and 40 minutes after taking off from Aero. I parked the Baron, arranged for heater maintenance the following day, rented a car and drove to Kent. We arrived there at about 11 p.m., just in time for the boys to check in.

10

FOUNDING
ANOTHER COMPANY

Building a new airport at Monroe

I won't go into all the bad reasons for my company, Allvac Metals, joining Vasco Metals, nor the only slightly better reasons for Allvac & Vasco then becoming a subsidiary of Teledyne, the California conglomerate. Suffice it to say that these mergers expanded my flying experiences and opened an opportunity to build a new airport in Allvac's hometown of Monroe, North Carolina.

Soon after Allvac merged with Vasco, I learned that George Roberts, Vasco's CEO, had wanted to buy a company plane for a long time. But since his directors were neither born nor raised in Silicon Valley, he could never get the subject on the table. At the first Vasco board meeting I attended, in Latrobe, Pennsylvania, after we merged, George asked me to try and soften up his board by rhapsodizing about why Allvac owned an airplane.

"Flying is second nature with us at Allvac," I explained to the assembled old gentlemen. "For example, I left my office at 5 yesterday, drove the short distance to Aero Plantation, where I keep the company Baron, and took off at 5:30. I landed two hours later here at the Latrobe airport, and we had drinks and a nice dinner together at the Vasco Lodge last evening.

"Otherwise, I would have had to spend an hour driving to the Charlotte airport and another hour flying from Charlotte to Pittsburgh. Then I would have had to rent a car and drive another two hours to Latrobe, getting here about midnight. The only safe part of the trip would have been the hours in the air! Of course, we would have missed the constructive, informal dinner meeting we are having here tonight.

"Every week that goes by, several Vasco officers, salesman and staff take that hazardous, two-hour car trip to catch a plane out of Pittsburgh. Avoiding the risk of that car trip alone, not to mention the lost time, could justify a small company plane," I concluded.

To head off the economic argument against flying, I looked directly at the Vasco treasurer, Ray Kelm, and said, "I don't know how to justify the expense of a company plane from the 'bean counter's' point of view. I know it pays but don't know how to prove it pays.

"You guys will be visiting us in Monroe fairly frequently now that we've merged." I continued. "I know that because we plan to take all your hard-earned cash that has been sitting in the Mellon Bank and invest it in new products and processes in Monroe. I know you say that we will continue to be free and autonomous, but I also know who will be signing the checks, and your cash will be flowing down South so fast, you'll want an airplane to keep up with it."

A month or two later, Arnold Palmer, who happened to be the famous Latrobe golfer, bought his first Learjet, and Vasco bought his used Aero Commander, along with the services of his two pilots. I think Palmer was glad to "Palm off" his used plane on Vasco, because Latrobe Steel, our hometown arch-competitor, retained Palmer to play golf with its customers, not Vasco's.

When he heard that Vasco had bought Palmer's used Commander, the Hawker Sidney jet salesman knew that, before long, Vasco would be a likely candidate for a jet. He called and offered George Roberts, president of Vasco, a demonstration flight from Latrobe to Charlotte, and George promptly accepted.

George called and asked me to meet him at Charlotte and to get checked out in the jet before we did any other company business, like investing still more of Vasco's money. This was my first chance to fly a jet. The captain put me in the left seat and, after 15 or 20 minutes of instruction, I took off and experienced the big difference between flying a jet and a Baron. After galloping down the runway, the instructor told me to rotate it and take off. I pulled the controls back to my chest and we headed for the sky, climbing at 4,000 feet per minute at an angle of 15 degrees.

I had a funny feeling in the pit of my stomach, such as I hadn't experienced since I was a kid, swinging in my yard 30 feet below the limb of a big oak tree. I flew the jet for half an hour, and the salesman took over the controls just before we landed. The salesman/pilot said he was sure he could check me out to solo in a few hours, but we had other business to do that day.

M y only other chance to fly a jet was when I leased a Learjet from Executive Aviation to fly from Chicago to Charlotte. The captain also put me in his left seat while he occupied the right seat, and he sent the co-pilot back to the cabin for a nap. The only problem I had was keeping the Mach 1 horn from sounding when I let the nose drift down too much and we approached the speed of sound!

Some months later, Ted Franks, an officer at Allvac and a director at Vasco, was with me when we got off to a late start from Aero Plantation for the monthly Vasco directors meeting in Latrobe. I had to file an IFR (instrument flight rules) flight plan because it was snowing over western Pennsylvania and we would arrive well after dark. It was clear sailing until we crossed the West Virginia/Pennsylvania state line.

One hundred miles south of Pittsburgh, flying at 10,000 feet, we were about 1,000 feet on top of a thick bank of snow clouds. Ground control called and said, "Expect severe icing conditions at 6,000 to 8,000 feet during your descent into Latrobe."

We flew on, and Ted constantly shined a flashlight, first to the right wing and then to the left wing, looking for any sign of ice. We could see none. In the 3,000-odd hours I had flown Beechcraft Barons, I'd experienced serious icing conditions only once. Luckily, that was when I was flying my first Baron, which had de-icing boots. At that time, I could pop off the ice from the wings and the tail simply by actuating the deicer, i.e. pumping up the rubber membranes on the leading edges of the wings and the tail. Since I'd used the deicing boots only 20 minutes in 1,000 hours, I didn't include them as an extra on this, my second Baron.

Since the shapes of the wings and tail are drastically altered by ice buildup, the "lift" of the wing and tail surfaces is markedly reduced. The stalling speed of the Baron can increase from the normal 70 mph to 100 mph. The added drag on the surfaces also drastically decreases the speed. And, of course, if the speed falls below the stalling speed, the plane will no longer fly. Obviously then, icing problems are close kin to thunderstorms, and pilots avoid both culprits like the plague.

I was really worried when ground control called and cleared me to descend to a lower altitude, approving a VOR instrument approach to the Latrobe airport. The standard VOR approach into Latrobe involves flying level at 3,000 feet, directly over the airport's VOR radio station. Then, holding altitude at 3,000 feet, you fly out eight miles on a set compass course, and make a standard, 180-degree turn back toward the VOR station while descending at 500 feet per minute. Flying the VOR approach would put me at an altitude of 500 feet over the threshold of the runway. My real worry: There were hills at 2,500 feet out near where the return is executed, and I wasn't keen on being out there while taking on a heavy load of ice. After hearing from the controller that there were no other planes in the control zone around Latrobe, I asked flight control to approve an alternate approach that wouldn't require wandering off into the Pennsylvania hills. My alternate plan was to set up a standard, 30-degree rate of turn and spiral directly down to the VOR station. I knew I would pass over the airport once on every 360-degree turn, and I shouldn't have any trouble finding the field when I broke out at the 2,000-foot reported cloud ceiling. I planned to speed up the descent to 1,000 fpm to minimize time for ice buildup while in the clouds. My mind was focused on getting out of this foreboding sky and onto *terra firma* as quickly as I could.

My alternate plan was approved, and as we passed over the VOR station, I set up a standard, 30-degree bank on the automatic pilot. I set the engines at 15 inches pressure and 1,500 rpm for a 2,000 fpm descent, and we spiraled into the clouds below. Ted Franks sat calmly beside me, listening to my radio conversations with controllers, who watched us on radar.

It seemed like forever, but it was only five minutes before we broke out of the clouds at about 1,000 feet above the Latrobe airport. It was a few seconds before crossing the VOR again, so when we looked down to the right there was a glorious sight: runway lights on solid ground.

The engines had cooled off while running at low power during the descent, and we had collected a heavy load of snow and ice not only all over the plane but also in the air intake duct on the engine cowlings. When we saw the lighted runway, I revved up the engines to 2,000 rpm and started to circle the field and prepare for a power landing. Suddenly, both engines coughed and sputtered, and I could feel that we had taken on a very heavy load of ice by the plane's sluggish response to the controls as I circled the field and lined up on the runway. I assumed that the ice load was so heavy that the plane would probably stall at 100 mph, so I was keeping it hot at 115 mph.

After the coughing engines had scared Ted and me out of our skins, both engines decided to run. I set them at 1,800 rpm, well above the normal 1,500 rpm approach power. I passed over the threshold of the runway 20 feet off the ground at 110 mph, 40 mph above normal stalling speed.

Ted Franks, who had bought a Beech Bonanza and taken up flying a year or so before, calmly said: "Jim! Do you realize you're landing downwind?"

I couldn't believe that my preoccupation in spiraling down through the ice had completely consumed my concentration, and I was about to land in the wrong direction on the active runway! Now I faced the critical decision: Should I risk going around with this load of ice on sputtering engines and make another approach from the right direction, or should I risk landing downwind with an eight-knot tail wind?

I couldn't imagine any other fool being up in this ice who would be sharing the runway with us, in either direction, and it was reassuring when ground control said that no other traffic was reported.

I chose to stay the course and continue the approach. The ice load was too great. At about 10 feet off the ground, as I was gingerly slowing the speed through 95 mph, the plane stalled and flat-out stopped flying. It dropped like a rock to the snow-covered runway.

I have never hit the ground so hard!

Fortunately, the landing gear held together. I canceled our IFR flight plan, and we taxied in to the ramp, parked and climbed out. Neither Ted nor I said a word, but we reveled in our safe silence.

Arnold Palmer's Learjet was sitting in his private, heated hanger a few hundred yards away. I parked our Baron in the snow and tied her down. The Vasco chauffeur was waiting to take us to the Vasco Lodge, where four ounces of scotch on the rocks calmed our nerves. On that night, I certainly would not have spoken on behalf of Vasco rushing out to buy an airplane!

While pounding the airways, I've been involved in only one near miss. It was real and it was scary. I was flying on an IFR south of the busy Newark airport in New Jersey. I was cleared by approach control to descend to 3,000 feet in the Newark traffic-control zone. The low, scattered clouds were open enough so that I was tempted to cancel my IFR as a United Airlines pilot flying just behind me had done. I was on the downwind leg approaching the airport, which was to my right.

As I traveled a few miles beyond the airport, the controller called,

"477 Alpha Papa cleared for a 180-degree right turn to intercept the ILS approach to runway 26."

Just before I completed the turn, in the clouds, and as I was ready to line up on the ILS, I broke out of the clouds and saw the same United pilot who had canceled his IFR plan. His plane was completing a turn on my left, ready to line up on the same ILS, to land on the same active runway. I would guess we were separated by about 200 feet, on a collision course! I ceased my turn so that I could come in behind the passenger plane.

"Is it he or me who has been approved for this airspace and to land on this runway?" I growled to the tower.

Immediately after that, the United pilot, who certainly had heard me and, hopefully, seen me, abruptly climbed at a steep angle above my path and flew away.

The tower responded to my inquiry, "477 Alpha Papa cleared for ILS approach."

After I landed and was passed off from the tower to ground control, I confirmed the near miss to the FAA at the Newark tower. They told me a car would pick me up after I parked and take me to the tower for a report. The car did pick me up — a half hour later — and by the time I got to the tower, the United pilot had left on another flight and wasn't available for a meeting about our near miss.

Later, the FAA sent me a transcript of the conversations between the tower and the local traffic, and it was exactly as I've described it. They didn't say what action, if any, was taken with the United pilot.

A few years after we merged Vasco and then Teledyne, Henry Singleton, Chairman of Teledyne, asked me to join his small staff and work full time on acquisitions.

"Okay," I said, "but that will mean even more flying, and I'm getting tired of working all day and filing a flight plan to fly home at night. I want to hire a full-time pilot and buy a jet."

Henry agreed with the full-time pilot but suggested we wait a while for the jet.

Earlier, when the Teledyne board approved my plans to build a new titanium plant and to locate it away from the Allvac plant, I saw a chance to shake the Monroe city and county fathers off their duffs and to build a new Monroe airport.

I had tried to promote this for years. I even ran for county commissioner, thinking I could boost the project effectively from that office, if by some remote chance I could be elected. But I made two fatal mistakes. I ran on the Republican ticket, and only one in 100 residents of Union County was Republican. Second, a new Monroe airport was my main campaign theme. I realized my political naiveté when my campaign manager set me straight.

"Jim, ain't five people in Union County that own an airplane. So you stick your mouth out promoting an airport and you gain five votes and lose 5,000."

My latest plan for an airport had more teeth than politics. Aero Plantation satisfied the personal flying interest of Kay and me, but it wasn't built to be a commercial airport. To satisfy the business interests of Monroe and Union County, particularly those of Allvac Metals and the new titanium plant I would build, we needed a real commercial airport in Union County. I could clearly see the importance of corporate flying. I also knew that a new airport with a jet-length runway should be high on the list for attracting other new industries to the area.

So I decided to set the stage by locating the new titanium plant near Monroe, and I was determined to have an airport next to it, even if I had to build it alone.

First, I bought 60 acres of land for the new titanium plant adjacent to an additional nice, flat 600 acres, all four miles west of Monroe. Second, with the help of Bill Adams at the local bank, we got an option on 400 acres adjoining the 60 I'd bought. Third, I hired an airport architect to design a 4,000-foot landing strip on 100 acres through the middle of the parcel.

I brought in Dick Dickerson, a formidable general contractor and owner of the old Monroe airport that was about to close, as a 50/50 partner. We exercised the options and bought all the land in a new venture-capital company I organized, appropriately called Ventures, Inc. Koy Dawkins, a lawyer, and Bob Morrison, Dickerson's chief pilot, were limited partners, and Dickerson and I were the general partners.

Now, with the political clout of Dick Dickerson, Bill Adams and bank president Ed Gaskins, whom we had invited to the party, we presented to Monroe Mayor Eddie Faulkner and the city council:

1) a complete airport design with assurance from the architect that the FAA would pay for it, and

2) we offered to sell to the city, at our cost, 100 acres of land through

the middle of our property for a new Monroe airport.

The City Council accepted our plans, and City Manager Jim Henkel picked up the ball. Under his guidance, a new Monroe airport finally was built next door to Teledyne's titanium plant. Later, Jim received the Monroe Man of the Year Award for the active role he played in getting the airport built.

I donated the unique reception building with the rotating beacon on top as a landmark for the place. But now that building can hardly be seen because so many new corporate hangers surround the strip at the active Monroe airport.

11

KAY RACES

The Powder Puff and Angel derbies

Kay joined the Ninety-Niners, the women's flying organization, when she learned that our neighbor, Kathy Davis, a
former airline stewardess and a pilot, was a member. The
Ninety-Niners sponsor an annual, all-woman cross-country race
called "The Powder Puff Derby."

Kay wanted to compete in the 1966 race, but she thought her
Cessna 150 was too slow for a cross-country flight. We traded Pete
Larson some land at Aero Plantation for his Cessna 182, and Kay
was ready to tackle the Powder Puff Derby race between Seattle,
Washington and Clearwater, Florida. The 182 was well equipped
for instrument flying, except that it had no automatic pilot.

Most pilots who race invite co-pilots to travel with them. With
two people flying, an automatic pilot isn't so important. But Kay
was flying solo, so we thought an autopilot was necessary for the
long, diagonal trip across the United States from Seattle to
Clearwater. We had an automatic pilot installed in the 182, and I
planned to accompany Kay on the trip from Charlotte. But the day
before we planned to leave Charlotte, the new autopilot still was
malfunctioning.

I called Cessna's home office in Wichita, Kansas, and told them
about the critical problem. They agreed to have a technician standing by to fix the autopilot during our overnight stop in Wichita.

Early on the morning of June 30, 1966, Kay and I climbed in and
took off for Kansas. With one gas stop in Illinois, we arrived at
Wichita at 3 p.m. as planned. The Cessna sales manager and two
technicians were waiting, and they fixed the autopilot before sun-
down.

We took off early the next morning with a smooth-functioning
autopilot, arriving at Seattle on July 1. The plane was checked in
and impounded until race time.

On July 2, I bid Kay *bon voyage* just before she climbed aboard and cranked her engine in the din stirred up by the planes of 56 other women. One by one, they taxied out and were off for the race to Clearwater.

I had some business with Boeing in Seattle, then hopped a commercial flight back to Charlotte. I picked up three of our children, Holly, Mary and Jack, in my Baron and we flew to Florida to meet Kay.

It was quite a thrill for us to stand on the pier at Clearwater and watch the Powder Puff Derby planes making their final approaches to the airport. We had a radio, so we monitored the tower and heard the pilots checking in one after another for two hours before hearing Kay's familiar voice announcing her arrival. We drove the short distance to the airport and greeted Kay after she had checked in with the Derby timers. We didn't hear until the next day that she had landed in 19th place.

The next day, I flew the Baron back home, while Mary, Holly and Jack flew back in the 182 with Kay. It was a three-hour ride in the Baron and a four-hour ride in the Cessna, so I was waiting for them when they landed at Aero Plantation.

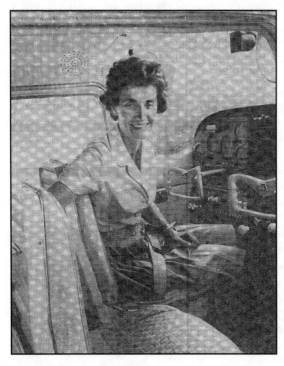

That evening, we celebrated with Kathy Davis and heard the details of Kay's cross-county race.

"I was so busy navigating and checking the winds aloft for the best altitude, I don't think I could have made it without the autopilot,"

Kay Nisbet at the controls.
-Collection of the Author

The Nisbets together in Clearwater, Fla., after the Powder Puff Derby race. From left are Holly, the Author, Kay, Jack and Mary.

-Collection of the Author

Kay declared. "It was a grueling flight. Always something to worry about: fuel, weather, the engine and me."

When Kay decided to enter two more races in 1967, we traded her 182 for a Piper Twin Comanche. It was owned by Curtis Turner, a Charlotte race-car driver. Kay hoped some of his racing luck would pass to her.

The first 1967 race was sponsored by another ladies' flying club, The Angels. The Angel Derby race was from Montreal to Miami. The second race, another Powder Puff Derby competition, was from Atlantic City, New Jersey, to Torrance, California, and was scheduled for June.

Kay was full of herself and bubbling with enthusiasm, telling me about her plans. She would be flying the faster twin Comanche and intended to leave a lot of other girls behind in turbulent headwinds.

The *Charlotte Observer* reported:

> *Is she nervous? Not exactly, though the prospect of flying 1,667 miles from Montreal to Miami all alone would immobilize most women.*

Flying to Kay Nisbet is as natural as breathing. After all, she was courted in a plane, by her husband James D. Nisbet, now an industrial executive. During the four years she's been flying she has compiled several hundred hours.

Even their life at a sprawling estate in Weddington (appropri-ately named Aero Plantation) revolves around flying: A soaring carport-hangar attached to their home houses planes as well as autos; a landing strip backs up to the house. Kay thinks nothing of flying over to Chapel Hill to pick up her son in school there or of flying any of the other three children around the country. She is chairman of the blood program in Union County and regularly delivers blood for the Mecklenburg County Red Cross. Recently she's flown in a visiting minister for her church and taken her Sunday school class members on a flying excursion (as a reward for learning the Ten Commandments.)

The thing I remember most about the Angel Derby is its dreary beginning. I was too busy at work to accompany Kay to Montreal, but I certainly remember when she left alone for the trip.

Mary, Holly and I walked with Kay to the hangar next to our house where "His and Hers" (His Baron and Her Comanche) were parked. It was a miserable, rainy day. Mary and Holly stood under umbrellas outside the hanger while I helped Kay aboard with her light luggage. Then I stood outside the hangar while she fired up the two engines and taxied out and down the road toward the land-ing strip. It was pouring and foggy.

Six or seven minutes later, we heard her at the other end of the strip, checking out the engines. We waited a few minutes while she was getting her IFR clearance by radio from Charlotte. Then we heard her "rev 'em up" and head down the strip. We peered through the gloom behind the hangar as she roared by, and we could see the landing gear retracting into the fuselage. I'm sure she couldn't see us waving goodbye because the Comanche disappeared into the soup as it passed the hanger, headed for Montreal, flying under instrument flight conditions, IFR, all the way, in soupy weather, all alone.

A couple of hours later, Kay called from Baltimore and said she had stopped to have a mechanic check out an unusual problem:

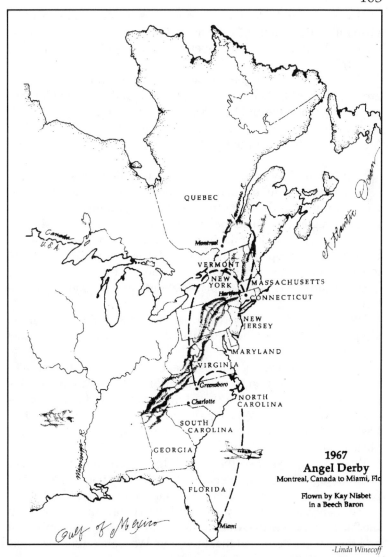

1967
Angel Derby
Montreal, Canada to Miami, Fl

Flown by Kay Nisbet
in a Beech Baron

-Linda Winecoff

The engines were racing when she switched from auxiliary fuel tanks back to the mains.

After dark, she called from Montreal to say the engine problem had been fixed. I asked her if the weather had improved. She said she'd been on instruments all the way and had made a nice ILS approach into Montreal in spite of exhaustion from the arduous flight.

"I was glad to learn that the controllers in Montreal spoke English rather than French," Kay said. "Remember that wake-up call I gave in French to the hotel operator in Paris and we didn't get called?"

"English is the standard language for controllers at airports around the world," I said. "Have a good time at Expo '67 in Montreal tomorrow. Goodbye and have a safe trip to Miami."

The weather improved and she completed the flight from Montreal to Miami without problems, coming in 10th in the race.

In July 1967, Kay flew her Twin Comanche alone to Atlantic City, the starting point of the next Powder Puff Derby race, this time to Torrance, Calif. That same day, I left Charlotte for some business in Oregon. She called me there the next night and said she was ready to leave for California the next morning. Kay called me again to say she had stopped off in Amarillo, Texas, to refuel and to spend the night. I flew down from Oregon to meet her the next day at the Torrance airport. Again, Kay placed about midway among the contestants.

We attended the Ninety-Niners banquet that night, but couldn't sleep very well. So we checked out of the hotel at 3 a.m. and headed for the airport.

We flew home together, across the fearful Rockies, the flat Midwestern plains, and on to the eastern Blue Ridge Mountains. We had flown this route half a dozen times before and had often included the passages in Washington and Oregon, the Columbia River Basin, and had flown between the snowcapped peaks of Hood, Shasta, Rainier and Adams.

When we approached the Blue Ridge Mountains in Tennessee late that night in cloudy, menacing weather, we had to file an IFR from the air and soar through solid soup for the last 200 miles.

Suddenly, after the very long and weary day all the way from the Pacific almost to the Atlantic, the clouds cleared. Stars appeared and the moon brightened the dim cabin. We were under the direction of Charlotte approach control, and they called our plane:

"Comanche 55AP, Aero Plantation strip straight ahead at 12:00, four miles."

I saw the dim lights on my backyard landing strip. The moon's reflection on Aero Plantation's dozen lakes looked like 100 acres of mirrors below. I responded to Charlotte control, "55AP, I have Aero

Plantation in sight, cancel instrument flight plan. Good night."
We landed and taxied to the security of home.

✟

"Lord, have mercy upon us
Christ, have mercy upon us
Lord, have mercy upon us"

✟

On August 27, 1967, a few weeks after we returned from the West Coast, Kay planned to fly to Danbury, Connecticut, to bring back our boys' favorite master, Lee Ahlborn, and his wife from Kent School for a long weekend. I called at about noon and caught her just before she left. I asked if she had checked the weather. She said she had, and it was okay going north, but later in the day there might be scattered cumulonimbus buildups and thunderstorms on the return trip.

When I got home at 6 p.m., Jack said the Danbury airport operator had called to tell me that Kay had left at 4:20 p.m. on an IFR flight plan and that it would be solid soup all the way. Lee and Babs Ahlborn were with her. She hoped to be back home about 7:30 p.m.

At 7:15, I took off from Aero in Kay's Comanche (Kay had flown in the faster Baron) and I monitored the Charlotte approach frequency. I planned to escort them into Aero Plantation. For 30 minutes I flew around, but 477AP never checked in with Charlotte approach control.

It was getting dark, so I landed back at Aero Plantation. Kay had said earlier that she would land at Charlotte rather than Aero if she arrived after dark. Jack and Jim drove to the Charlotte Airport to wait.

At 9 p.m., there still was no word, but I held an open line to the Charlotte airport tower. I thought to myself: She must have landed, but deep inside I knew she hadn't because she would have called. I thought she had deviated miles around a storm, but I knew by now that her five hours of fuel would be gone.

Despair gripped me. Kay was now overdue by two hours. I paced the floor.

The phone rang and I grabbed it, hoping for good news but sensing bad.

"Mr. Nisbet?"

"Yes."

"This is the coroner in Lancaster, Pennsylvania. A Baron 477AP cracked up in a severe thunderstorm over Lancaster. All three aboard were killed."

Holly, listening in on the conversation, realized what had happened and began to cry. I told the boys at Charlotte to come straight home; that their mother had landed at Lancaster, Pennsylvania. They sensed what had happened, too.

Mary was at a horseback-riding camp in the mountains. I called, and her councilor, a close family friend, promised to drive her home at once.

Unexpectedly, my brother Oliver and his wife walked into the house: They had heard the bad news from the Union County Sheriff's Department. They were afraid I'd been on board, too. Early the next morning, our friend Lindsay Hess flew Oliver and his son Johnny to Lancaster, and returned to Aero about sunset. I met the plane. In the back seat was a plastic sack tied with a string.

"My God! It can't be!" I shouted.

Oliver hustled me away, and Lindsay Hess took off for Atlanta for the cremation. The next day, he returned with an urn of ashes in a velvet bag. A few hundred people came to extend sympathy. I met them all with tranquilized and blurry eyes. At night, I walked alone in the woods, and I cried aloud beneath the pines, maples and oaks. I pleaded with God for Kay's return, just for a day.

The funeral followed two days later, and the ashes were interred at the Nisbet family plot at the old Waxhaw Cemetery in South Carolina, beside my dad and my sister, Nancy.

What now but the lonely realization that the courage required for all my achievements were not solo, but derived in great measure from the courage and wisdom, the belief and derring-do of Kay Nisbet.

The following transcript, provided to me by the FAA, was recorded by the New York Flight Control Centers:

Kay to New York Control: *"Baron 477AP off Danbury at 4:18 p.m. Climbing direct to Carmel."*

New York Control: *"477AP, radar contact. Cleared direct to Carmel. Climb to 8,000, report leaving 6,000."*

A few minutes later, Kay responded:

"477AP at 6,000, on instruments in solid clouds."

New York Control: *"477AP Roger. Change frequency to 126.8."*

Kay on 126.8: *"477AP at 8,000. Clouds broken, rising cumulus ahead. Slight turbulence."*

New York Control: *"Roger, radar contact."*

Kay was approaching the busiest sector in the New York control zone. Weather was rapidly deteriorating. The ground controller in this sector was as busy as a cat on a hot tin roof trying to sort out incoming traffic from the west to the New York area. Other private pilots and airline captains vied for alternate clearances from the ground controller, and traffic was backing up west across Pennsylvania.

New York Control called a United Airlines captain: *"United 483, hold at 12,000 over Lancaster."*

United 483 responded: *"Negative. My on-board radar is painting severe weather over Lancaster. I am 20 miles west in the clear but can see a thunderstorm rising to 30,000 feet ahead. I request to hold at present position.*

New York Control: *"United 483, approved."*

Another of the many airlines in the control zone was Eastern. New York Control called Eastern: *"Eastern 87, New York Control calling!"*

The Eastern captain responded: *"New York Control, don't talk to me now. I'm in severe turbulence in the middle of a storm and am headed out westward at 270 degrees."*

A few minutes later, Eastern called and reported a western course, requesting a hold at Harrisburg at 10,000 feet, which was granted. Then a private pilot broke through the continuous radio chatter, and the tone of his voice was dead serious:

"Cessna 310C to New York Control, at 6,000, 20 miles northeast of Lancaster. Severe turbulence. Request clearance for immediate descent to a lower altitude."

New York Control: *"Cessna 310C, cleared to descend to 3,000 — await landing clearance."*

At this time, New York Control was well aware of the storm over Lancaster and Kay's flight path in 477AP, which had no on-board radar.

New York Control: *"477AP, are you okay?"*

Kay: *"477AP — I guess so. Solid soup, raining torrents, severe turbulence."*

Later, when Kay could break into the cluttered chatter, she requested:

"477AP — *Request deviation 10 left. Extreme turbulence."*

New York Control: "477AP, *10 left of course approved."*

Kay didn't acknowledge, and for five minutes New York Control called her with no response. They finally suggested she change frequency to 122.6, Lancaster Flight Service. Then New York Control called Lancaster Flight Service by telephone and both frantically tried to contact 477AP.

New York Control: "477AP, *radar contact lost, call Lancaster Flight Service on 122.6, 122.6. Do you read? 477AP - do you read New York?"*

There was no response.

12

WHEN THROWN FROM A HORSE...

Climb back on and fly again!

It was some weeks before the therapeutic effects of all the rituals that follow a death subsided. My life continued. I couldn't get off. My daughters, Mary and Holly, and my sons, Jim and Jack, climbed into Kay's Comanche with me and we flew to Pawley's Island, on the South Carolina coast, to spend a few days with my brother Oliver and his wife, Ida. It was a strange feeling, flying in Kay's Comanche, the plane she and I had so recently flown from California, back home to Aero Plantation after her race across the country.

The Comanche had been parked beside the Baron at Aero Plantation when Kay chose the faster Baron to fly to Connecticut. I couldn't help but wonder: If she had flown the Comanche instead of the Baron, could it have withstood the severe turbulence better? Or would the slower speed have put the Comanche a mile or perhaps five miles away from the bolt of lightning that struck the Baron?

The sun and the sounds of the sea were good therapy, but I eventually learned that only the passage of time could sort of heal the wounds left by Kay's death. And the scars will remain forever.

The week after we returned from the shore, the Cessna dealer in Charlotte called and said he would like to park a new Cessna 310 at my strip for my free use until I replaced my plane. For a long time he had tried to get me to trade my Baron for a Cessna 310.

Now when the Beech dealer heard about this, *he* parked a new *Baron* at the end of my strip, right beside the Cessna, also for my free use until the insurance company replaced my plane with what they called an "equivalent plane." It could have been a Cessna 310 if I had wanted to switch makes.

It seemed pretty ridiculous to have this option of three light twins:

a Cessna, a Baron and a Comanche. I flew the 310 for several hours during the next few weeks, but after flying a Baron for so long, I wasn't comfortable in anything else. In fact, I was beginning to realize that I would never completely relax flying a small plane again. But flying and trading airplanes was too much in my blood to give up.

The insurance company called and said they had found a Baron with fewer hours on the engines and better-equipped in several ways. It had a better transponder and a radio altimeter that enabled traffic controllers to monitor the altitude, but it didn't have de-icing boots. I accepted it as a fair replacement for my lost ship.

The Cessna salesman was disappointed when he flew his demonstrator away. I called Lindsay Hess, and he flew the Comanche to Rock Hill, and sold it a short time later.

I took off from Aero Plantation in the new Baron in late November 1967. I was flying at 10,500 feet on top of scattered clouds. I could see far into the distance. To my left and right, cumulinimbus clouds rose to 30,000 feet. I kept my distance from their thunder and lightning — turbulence that can take off a wing in a flash.

After a long flight, thoughtful but uneventful, I landed in Toronto. The new plane had functioned well: It ran like a top.

My mission in Toronto was to buy an old iron foundry. An iron foundry isn't very exciting, but in the conglomerate decade of the 1960s, Teledyne was buying just about anything if it was cheap enough. It didn't matter what the target company made: We couldn't turn down buying a company for 10 times earnings if we could pay for it in Teledyne stock priced at 60 times earnings. Turning a real value of $1 into a Wall Street value of $6 was the name of the game.

Looking back at that era, the amazing thing was that the conglomerate formula worked so well for so long. We didn't take into serious account the fact that we would, in time, eventually be cheapening Teledyne by buying cheap companies. Nevertheless, two days after I arrived, the mission was accomplished.

As I prepared to leave Canada, the weather was terrible, with a 500-foot ceiling and drizzle. Worse yet, a 400-foot ceiling was reported for Charlotte. It's not much fun to do business all day, then have to worry about weather while flying back home alone after dark. I filed a non-stop instrument flight plan back to Charlotte, and after the standard ground inspection and instrument and engine cockpit checks, I revved her up and headed down the runway, mentally preparing to shift from VFR to IFR when I hit the clouds a few hundred feet after lift-off.

Just before entering the soup, the right door flew open! I immediately throttled back the engines, told the control tower my problem, and circled back to land. The Beech Baron is a fine, small, twin-engine plane, but every Baron I've flown has had a virus in the door-lock mechanism. A good mechanic familiar with the problem fixed the door lock in a few minutes.

I was anxious to head south and hoped to reach Charlotte before dark, thinking about the reported 400-foot ceiling there. After renewing my clearance for the IFR flight, I taxied out, took off and hit the soup at 600 feet. I didn't break out into clear skies on top at 8,000 or 9,000 feet as I'd expected. I still was in solid soup even after climbing to 12,000 feet! I didn't want to fly any higher because I hadn't yet equipped this plane with oxygen. I leveled off at 10,000 feet and set the autopilot to hold that altitude. I got out my Jeppson charts (maps for aircraft navigation) to restudy the instrument approaches at Charlotte and settled down for a long, rainy flight.

I'd been flying level at 10,000 feet, listening to the rain pound against the windshield, when the worst of all experiences in flying occurred: I smelled smoke!

It was horrifying. My number one navigation and communication radio, nav-com, began crackling. There was a stronger burning odor in the cabin, then silence. The radio had failed. That was certainly unnerving, but I knew I had a backup nav-com radio. I tuned it in on the Pittsburgh VOR and reset the autopilot to track on the #2 nav-com.

That worked, and all was well — for another 10 minutes. Then I smelled smoke *again*, and heard a crackling sound similar to the death throes of #1. And #2 died!

I turned my radar transponder to the standard emergency frequency. I carefully noted the time and my present position, and I began to sweat. Under such conditions, the instrument flight rules call for staying the course on the last approved flight plan, which was to Charlotte. At least ground controllers could follow my course by following my transponder signals, assuming the transponder hadn't failed, too.

The transponder is one of the best, relatively new, navigation instruments for aircraft. It sends out continuous radio signals at frequencies specified by ground control and set by the pilot. The signal is received by ground control and is converted to a "blip" on the controller's radar screen. Controllers can follow the plane continuously. If the plane has a radio altimeter as the Baron did, controllers can keep track of its altitude as well.

But with the loss of both nav-com radios, I had no radio communication at all. I still was two hours from Charlotte. If I had to fly by the magnetic compass alone, I'd be lucky even to find North Carolina.

In all my years of flying, I'd never used the oldest radio on the instrument panel, the ADF. It's much like a household radio fitted with a special compass that points directly toward the radio station it's tuned to. I turned it on and it worked! I tuned in to an AM frequency at 1010, WBT radio in Charlotte. It came in loud and clear. By adjusting my direction to zero on the ADF compass, I knew I was headed straight for WBT in downtown Charlotte.

When I was a boy, I'd lived just across the South Carolina state line from Charlotte, and the sound of WBT now comforted me like a long-lost friend.

Growing up, I'd listened to "Amos and Andy" on WBT. In spite of the fix I was in, one Amos and Andy story I'd heard many years before flashed through my mind: The guys had chosen a place to meet at noon the following day.

"Now if you get there first, you make a mark, and if I get there first, I'll rub it out," Amos told Andy.

I cruised on, getting wetter with sweat, my mouth as dry as a cinder. I said a little prayer, "Lord, God Almighty, I believe you have it in for me and are punishing me beyond reason. Please help me, though sinner I am. I swear I will start to go back to church next Sunday, and I will kneel, and I will pray, and I thank you in advance."

The rain finally lessened and the sky became brighter. About 100 miles from Charlotte I broke out clear on top, still with solid clouds beneath. I didn't know whether or not the ceiling in Charlotte had lifted.

Twenty miles out, a few breaks appeared in the clouds, and I saw a large cemetery below. That's the Gospel truth.

Now I had at least a 1,000-foot ceiling under broken clouds. Down I soared, and the Charlotte tower had a green light out, clearing me to land. Ground controllers had followed me all the way, thanks to the transponder, which, fortunately, along with the blessed ADF, kept functioning.

As it turned out, the outside thermometer wire that passes through the windshield hadn't been properly sealed, and my radios had shorted out in the rain. I went home, but Kay wasn't there to share my latest exciting flying experience.

I continued to work for Teledyne for another year and resigned in 1970, after the era of conglomerate acquisitions dried up. I retired for about a month, then hung out my shingle as a money manager, returning to work full time.

I used the Baron only twice to fly for the new business. Once, my partner and I flew to visit a rich fellow in Greenville, S.C. We had handled his bond account for nearly a year and our performance had been unusually good.

Our grateful client congratulated us and said, "Since you can't possibly do an encore, I'm taking my money back!"

The other trip we took was to Wilmington, N.C., where I had to make a very rusty ILS instrument approach. We had flown there on a fateful visit to interview and sign on two young chemists from DuPont who had developed a "foolproof," computer-based program for investing in common stocks. In the crash of 1972, the partnership we made with them temporarily did in our money-management business and proved their "foolproof" system had made fools of us.

13

A NEW PASSENGER

And flying here, there and yon

Afew strange things happened when I was a lonesome widower, mainly because flying offers broad possibilities to fulfill that ancient craving that nature provided to all humankind, that search for companionship, the desire to hold another person, the longing for the climactic fulfillment of the loving process.

Hemingway likened it to "when the ground moves."

After four or five months, I called a recently widowed lady friend in Charlotte and asked her to dinner. Unlike me, she had been widowed long enough to have passed the worst of her bereavement and had returned to something like normality.

Maybe we could share our loneliness, I thought.

I picked her up at about dark at her home and we returned to Aero Plantation, not to my home, but to my Baron next door. She was an inexperienced flyer, especially when it came to private flying after dark in my kind of style for this special night.

We climbed aboard and I fired up the engines, taxied to the strip, turned on the navigation and instrument lights, and clicked the frequency to turn on the runway lights. I taxied to the end of the strip, turned around, checked the engines and gave her full throttle. We roared down the runway, lifted off, wheels-up, throttled back, into the star-filled, moonlit sky.

"Would you like to have dinner at the Country Club of North Carolina at Pinehurst?" I asked the startled, middle-aged lady.

"Well," she replied, "I'll settle for any option to this! I've never been lifted off the ground so quickly and with such flair; I'm very excited, and scared to death!" she exclaimed.

Nothing more was said for a long time. I could feel her fear subsiding. Then she relaxed and moved against me, closer, in the already snug cabin. "I'd love to have dinner at, where is it? Oh, the Country Club of North Carolina. A few glasses of wine and a little time might re-establish my appetite," she purred.

It was only a 25-minute flight from my strip at Aero Plantation to the Southern Pines airport. A car from the Country Club met us, and I'd already made reservations for dinner for two. I knew the waitress and the *maitre d'*. It was a weeknight, the dining room wasn't crowded and the service was excellent. The food was good, as usual, the wine mellowed our spirits and our companionship glowed. We were excited, we were dreaming.

After a two-hour dinner, we were chauffeured back to the airport and climbed into the Baron for the flight home. After we took off, I flew east rather than west toward Charlotte. At a cruising altitude of 5,500 feet, I switched on the autopilot and slowed the plane to 150 knots.

We chatted about flying. She knew a lot about astronomy and she identified stars. While we shared this unique experience, unconscious of time, the Atlantic Ocean appeared 20 miles ahead.

I turned 180 degrees and headed toward home. By this time, things had grown very cozy between us and she was no longer edgy about the flight. She had realized that the automatic pilot worked and that flying didn't require the use of my hands.

I lowered the arm-rests between us, reached across her and unlatched the control handle so the back of her seat could recline to a horizontal position. The automatic pilot was taxed to maintain control as "the ground moved."

I finally understood what my old friend Jim Russell had meant when he'd asked if I was a member of the "Mile High Club."

Jean and Dick Fairley were very close friends when Kay and I had lived in Schenectady, New York. They later became good friends with Margy and Perry Hazard, who moved to Schenectady after we had headed south. Later, after both Kay and Perry had passed away before their times, Jean called me and whetted my curiosity with her description of Margy Hazard, the young widow. But Jean, a proper, upper New York State lady, said I shouldn't get too interested yet.

"Wait a few months," she advised.

Three months later, Jean, the matchmaker, called and gave me Margy's telephone number. I promptly called, and Margy accepted my invitation to dinner, only after she rechecked with Jean to find out more about this guy from North Carolina. Dick got on the phone and told Margy she was old enough to make her own decision about a dinner date. Margy was 45 and I was 50.

She agreed to meet me at the Westchester, N.Y., airport the following Saturday, a 20-minute ride down the Merritt Parkway south of her home in New Canaan, Connecticut.

When Saturday came, the weather was horrible, and I decided to go commercial rather than fly my Baron on instruments, in solid scud, from Charlotte to Westchester. I still was gun shy about flying blind and not being able to see thunderstorms that might be lurking in the cumulonimbus clouds. I called Margy and told her I would fly commercial, get a limousine at LaGuardia Airport and meet her in New Canaan.

Before I arrived, Margy told her next-door neighbor that I was coming for dinner.

"Nobody in his right mind would fly into LaGuardia in this weather."

Later, when Margy told her I was on my way by limousine from LaGuardia, her neighbor responded, "You told me he's a Southerner, so I'll run down to the liquor store and get some dry mash bourbon. I know you don't stock that stuff, but that's what he'll want to drink."

I landed at LaGuardia two hours late, after a bumpy flight, and an approach that broke out under the clouds at 200 feet over the threshold of the runway. My limousine was the last one to cross the Triborough Bridge before it was closed because of high winds. I finally arrived at New Canaan and called Margy from the midtown Exxon station; I told her she would recognize me as the only man there wearing a green leather overcoat. She later said how nervous she'd been about meeting a stranger in a green leather overcoat. I think she had visions of me standing by a Harley-Davidson motorcycle!

"After such a bad trip, would you like something to drink?" Margy soon asked.

"Thanks. How about a vodka on the rocks?" I replied.

For the next several months, I was able to adjust my business flying to include frequent visits to New Canaan and dates with Margy. We talked about the possibility of a future together and we wondered if our children would make good stepchildren. I think Margy was particularly concerned about her transition from a Connecticut Yankee to a Southern lady. That didn't bother me because I had made the geographical, South to North, transition a long time ago and I knew about "them Yankees."

Margy and I had our first long flight in the Baron when we flew from Westchester to Naples, Florida, to visit Margy's mother. We planned an overnight stop at Aero Plantation so she could meet Mary and Holly.

The night before we left, Margy had entertained a group of ten of her best friends at a dinner party in her home in New Canaan. Among the guests were Sue and Guthrie Spears. Guthrie was a prominent minister, pastor of the First Presbyterian Church there.

Margy asked me to sit at the head of the table and carve the turkey, a sure signal to the gathering that she was eyeing me quite seriously as a potential mate. But she forgot to tell me that there were a few antiques on which I wasn't supposed to sit. After everybody else was seated, and I had held the chair for Sue Spears, I pulled back the chair at the head of the table and sat down, but I didn't stop when my bottom reached the chair! The old thing collapsed and broke into smithereens, and I went sprawling on the floor. The men at the table sprang to my aid. The ladies wondered about this Southern fellow.

Early the following morning, the weather reports were good: widely scattered clouds, visibility unlimited, winds aloft out of the southwest at 18 knots and forecast to be stronger at our planned cruising altitude of 10,500 feet, VFR all the way.

When we taxied out toward the active runway at the busy Westchester airport, I pointed out to Margy the dozens of corporate jets being pulled from their private hangers and parked on the tarmac, waiting for the CEOs of American business to be flown to the next town, the next state, across the country or abroad. Their well paid pilots knew the way to anywhere.

For Margy's continuing education, I was mouthing my actions as we flew. When the control tower cleared us for take-off, I revved up the two 285-hp Continental engines to full throttle and, with only one passenger, we were off the ground after a run of 1,000 feet. After flicking the "wheels-up" switch for the retractable landing gear, I followed the standard procedure for climbing out: throttle set back to 25 inches, manifold pressure and props adjusted for 2,500 rpm, fuel switched from mains to auxiliary tanks, navigation radio and heading set on OMNI transmitter at the VOR station at Harrisburg, Pennsylvania (first leg south, 110 miles away). I switched on the automatic pilot to take us toward the VOR station.

We relaxed and headed for 10,500 feet, my chosen altitude for the VFR flight. The only remaining work while climbing to cruising altitude was to advance the throttle periodically. This was to maintain 25 inches manifold pressure to compensate for the pressure loss because of thinning air as we climbed. Engine speed was set at 2,500 rpm by adjusting the pitch of the props.

About 10,000 feet is the ideal altitude for the Baron's performance. It's a compromise between loss of power from less air intake and loss of wind resistance or drag because of less atmospheric resistance. With altitude reached, I set the engines only once more for the southward cruise, 23 inches manifold pressure and 2,300-rpm speed.

For the rest of the flight, the only work left was navigation — and keeping an eye peeled for other aircraft.

While cruising south across Pennsylvania, I explained to Margy the purpose of each instrument and switch on the panel. I think the only ones she remembered forever afterward were the two fuel gauges. I unwisely told her about an engine failure I'd once had 20 miles south of Harrisburg. I quickly realized I was doing more than just making casual conversation, I was scaring the be-Jesus out of her! But by then, I had to finish the story and tell her about the safe end of that little episode.

I told her that just before landing on that occasion, I saw that the runway was surrounded by fire trucks. I asked the tower if there had been an accident.

"*You* declared an emergency when you called in and told us you had an engine failure and requested radar vectors direct to the airport!" the tower replied. "It's our standard procedure to alert the emergency equipment to stand guard. They're by the runway waiting for you to arrive."

"Gee. For me?" I said.

I made a perfectly good, easy landing with only one engine running. On a twin-engine plane, when one engine is lost, it takes only a little more rudder to control the landing, otherwise it's not a big deal. People fly on one engine all the time in single-engine planes! But the feeling is different when flying a twin on one fan.

Two hours into the flight, when Margy and I were cruising over

Virginia, Margy noticed that the two fuel gauges were bouncing off zero. I explained to her that it was standard practice not to switch from the auxiliary tanks back to the mains until the auxiliaries were empty. This procedure ruled out any thought of ever switching back to the auxiliaries if the mains ran low.

As I explained the reason, the left engine coughed and stopped. Margy had a conniption fit! I quickly switched back to the main tanks and the left engine sprang back to life. I didn't wait for the right engine to sputter and die, fearing Margy might jump out of the plane, so I switched the right engine to the right main tank, knowing that the auxiliaries had only a minute or two of fuel left.

This trip was extraordinary in other ways, too. The purpose of the stop at my home was to introduce Margy to my two daughters. Fortunately, they and Margy seemed to get along quite well, but I didn't dare ask for their specific stamp of approval for this prospective step-mother. A few weeks later, I did corral them for a meeting, as I often did after Kay left us, when there was something momentous to talk about.

No sooner had we gathered, when Mary said, "Pop, Holly and I have figured out what this meeting is all about. You want to tell us you and Margy plan to be married."

These two hadn't missed a trick. I had no way of reading the inner thoughts of my two teen-aged daughters, but I did feel like they thought it might be for the best — to settle me down at home. I suspected, but never knew until we talked about it years later, the very deep hurt and grief they both felt for many years after Kay's accident.

The flight on to Florida had another purpose: I was supposed ask Margy's mother for her hand and her blessing before we could be married. At the age of 50, I thought that was a bit much.

We flew past widely scattered, billowing cumulonimbus clouds all the way from Aero Plantation to Naples, arriving on a Friday afternoon. Margy's mother was a charming lady who never met anybody but a friend. Margy's step-father was a handsome and friendly gentleman. He still received royalties from tunes he'd written many years before while attending the University of Pennsylvania. He would spring into a song on a moment's notice, and he was an ardent golfer —— they made a great couple.

For the entire weekend, Margy never broached the subject of my looming conference with Mom, and I certainly didn't want to break that ice. But since nothing was said before I was ready to depart Monday morning, I went to Margy's mother and blurted it out.

"Gaga," (I thought it prudent to call her what her grandchildren called her.) "Will you give me Margy's hand and bless our marriage?"

Gaga responded with her usual bounding enthusiasm.

"Why, Jim, of course I will! I'm thrilled with the idea, and very happy about your plans. I was afraid you'd never ask!"

Margy stayed in Naples for a week, then stopped off in Charlotte for the weekend before returning to Connecticut.

Mary, Holly and I took Margy to the service at our small Episcopal church in Monroe on Sunday morning. When the usher passed the plate by our seat, I put in a dollar. At Margy's church, it was the custom to pass the plate on down the row, where another usher would receive it, step back and pass it to the first person in the next row behind. When she tried to take the plate, the alarmed usher held onto it.

Margy pulled harder.

The usher pulled harder, for several go-rounds, then finally let go. All the bills and loose change scattered on the floor between the two rows of seats! Holly, Mary and Margy got down on the floor and collected the lost loot. Red-faced, they returned it to the shaken usher, who proceeded up the aisle, gingerly holding the plate in and pulling it out as he passed each row.

It was communion Sunday. The same unfortunate usher moved up the aisle from the front to the back of the church, releasing communicants pew by pew. When he arrived at our row and stopped, signifying that we were next to go, Mary, Holly and I stood up, and I stepped into the aisle.

Margy sat like a post.

I motioned for her to stand and join me. Holly and Mary did, too. She just sat there. Holly and Mary stepped past her and joined me and we walked forward, took communion and returned to our seats. When we left the church, greetings and introductions in the yard were strained indeed. I was pretty mad.

When we finally made our way to the car and headed for home, Margy told us why she hadn't joined us for communion. When she was on the floor picking up the change, both slip straps had broken! She didn't want to totally embarrass us by losing her slip while walking down the aisle to take communion!

Margy and I were married in April 1969 and honeymooned in Bermuda, then settled at Aero Plantation. My manager there, James Richards, had the nine-hole golf course in pretty good shape, so we decided to have the party of all parties, an Aero Plantation Open.

We invited 150 people from Weekapaug, Rhode Island, where Margy's summer home was, from Charlotte and Monroe and from Ponte Vedra, Fla. Dick Fairley was put in charge of the golf tournament. We engaged a local barbecue chef to roast a pig for the occasion. I signed on the popular Charlotte band "Loomis McGoomus" to play, and my opera-singing pilot friend, Lindsay Hess, was the soloist. Tables were set with candelabra and flowers in the hangar by the landing strip.

Just as the sun sank and darkness was falling, Lindsay made a low pass and buzzed the crowd, zooming back up in a high vertical turn before cutting the power and gliding down to land at Aero. He taxied up to the edge of the hangar, cut the engines and climbed out of my Baron. He stood there in a beautiful white, double-breasted suit with his thick, curly, blond hair combed back in a pompadour. I introduced him.

"Lindsay will sing grace, the Lord's Prayer," I announced.

Lindsay sang the Lord's Prayer as it had never been sung before, and our guests' eyes were teary. Following the barbecue dinner, he sang an ending grace with my favorite song from *Porgy and Bess*, — "Summertime."

This was the grandest production I've ever put on, and friends who were there still talk about it. It was a fitting christening for Margy at Aero Plantation. I felt ready for Hollywood!

In August, the first summer after we married, friends of Margy invited us to visit them at Nantucket, Massachusetts. At the time, we were vacationing in Weekapaug. The day we took off for the short flight from the nearby Westerly, R.I., airport, the weather was crystal clear, visibility was unlimited, VFR all the way. Remember, VFR means "visual flight rules," see and be seen, and we could see and be seen for miles and miles on this beautiful summer day.

As we climbed out from Westerly, we could see Fishers Island, N.Y., to the west, Block Island to the south and Long Island to the

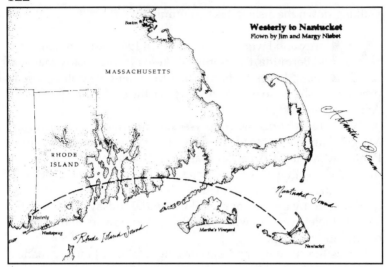

Westerly to Nantucket
Flown by Jim and Margy Nisbet

-Linda Winecoff

southwest, next to the Sound, all exactly where they belonged. After climbing a few thousand feet over the edge of the Atlantic, we
had traveled beyond the Port Judith lighthouse and could see,
slightly to the northeast, the summertime mansions of the
Vanderbilts, the Mellons, the Rockefellers and Jackie Kennedy at
Newport. There they rested in their weathering and withering splen-
dor.

At 6,500 feet, our cruising altitude, we unexpectedly hit some
severe, clear-air turbulence. We didn't see another plane, but that
kind of turbulence could only have come from the powerful, cy-
clone wake trailed by the four 50,000-pound-thrust engines of a
Boeing 747, cruising in from Europe and descending from Newfoundland, headed into New York's JFK to unload 400 tired souls.
On second thought, it could have been the cyclonic disturbance that
trails the Concorde, having just reduced its speed to below super-
sonic as it approached the coastline, hurtling in from either Paris or
London.

We flew on across Martha's Vineyard. A few minutes later, we
landed at Nantucket. We spent a pleasant evening and night with
friends on the quaint old island, a gathering place for New York
celebrities, writers and starlets, "Down Easters."

The next morning, the weather was in pronounced contrast to
that of the day before. Fog had rolled in, and the weather was hu-

mid, sultry and carried a New England misery. Solid, rainy soup covered the ocean, the cloud ceiling was only 600 feet and visibility less than a mile.

Our friends dropped us off at the airport. I checked the oil and had all four fuel tanks topped off. I filed an instrument flight plan back to Westerly with an estimated time of departure at 11 a.m. I started the engines and taxied out to the active runway. Ground control cleared us to take off, to follow the flight plan as filed. Once off, just after "wheels up," we quickly hit solid clouds, confirming that the reported ceiling surely was no more than 600 feet. Flying instantaneously shifted from VFR to IFR, from see and be seen to nothing to see and can't be seen, and, of course, the ground disappeared from sight.

IFR was a new experience for Margy. She was nervous — distraught, in fact — and she has never been more decisive.

"I can't see the ground! Land. Please land!" she shouted.

"Where, Margy? Please tell me where!" I answered.

All pilots have a healthy respect for bad-weather flying, and I suspect many pilots have a secret fear of flying in the soup. I probably do. The fear isn't so great that it deters them from practicing the trade. But watch any pilot when he sees a bad-weather report on TV, or hears a plane overhead when it's foggy outside, and he'll become as alert as a gun-shy hunting dog sniffing the wind and knowing a thunderstorm is coming.

On one of my frequent trips to Toronto, I asked Margy if she would like to go along so we could be together on my scheduled stop-off for an annual physical at the Greenbriar Hotel Clinic in West Virginia. The three-day physical at the Greenbriar allows time for golf, part of a healthy plan, you understand.

"IFR or VFR?" Margy wisely asked.

"The long-range forecast doesn't call for any bad weather in the Northeast, but nobody can guarantee the weather," I replied warily.

Off we flew from Aero Plantation to Toronto, clear skies, VFR all the way. After spending the night and completing my business by 3 p.m. the next day, we rushed to the Toronto airport, hoping to reach the Greenbriar before dark. The approach there is a narrow corridor between the mountains. I like daylight and good weather for that kind of approach.

I checked the oil and fuel, and we climbed aboard. My habit was to start the left engine first. When I switched on the starter for the right engine, it was as dead as a doornail. I shut down the left engine and we climbed out. I asked the line boy to fetch a mechanic as soon as possible. The mechanic quickly diagnosed the problem as a failed soldered joint in the starter cable. I suppose the Baron engine could have been propped, but Joe Lewis wasn't around to help. The mechanic couldn't fix it before noon the following day.

I went to the general aviation office nearby and asked for a charter flight, to leave as soon as possible. The only plane available was a single-engine Cessna 182. We climbed aboard with a young pilot who looked to be 16, and we took off for West Virginia, leaving the Baron behind.

By this time, it was past 4 p.m. The flight in the Baron would have taken about two hours, but in the slower plane it would be nearly three hours, putting our estimated time of arrival down that narrow corridor into the Greenbriar airport sometime after dark.

All went well until we were 50 miles south of Pittsburgh, when we found ourselves on top of a solid bank of clouds. I could tell that the young pilot was getting nervous. When it started to get dark, he began stuttering. I thought I'd better try to help him on what we were about to confront: an instrument landing in the mountains of West Virginia.

I asked him where he had gotten his instrument rating.

"I d-don't have an instrument rating," he stammered.

I couldn't believe it and had no ready reply! A fixed-base operator at Toronto had sent us off on this three-hour trip with a green pilot with the prospect of landing in West Virginia after dark.

The young pilot said, "You fly a Baron, so you must be instrument rated. I think you'd better take over."

I took the controls at once so I at least could get familiar with this plane before facing what lay ahead. In the past, Kay had owned a Cessna 182 Skymaster, but the last time I'd flown it was six or eight years before.

As sunset approached, I went through some familiarization procedures. I set up a glide path and refreshed my memory about the engine settings for a descent rate of 500 feet per minute, which I'd use for the let-down and the approach to the airport. I did three stalls to remind myself about the stalling speed for landing. Finally, I glued my eyes to the instrument panel and took a refresher cram-course in instrument flying a Cessna 182 with no autopilot.

The pilot hadn't even filed a flight plan, so I filed an instrument flight plan from the air without revealing our plight to the ground controller. I planned to wait until we started the let-down into the Greenbriar airport. Then I'd ask to be monitored by a ground controller and be given radar vectors and altitudes all the way down.

After filing the flight plan, ground control called and said, "Radar contact, 20 miles north, descend to 4,000 feet and switch frequency to the tower."

I throttled back the engine, and set up my 500-fpm rate of descent. As I picked up the microphone to acknowledge the new frequency and tell the control tower my problem, I looked below and, in the twilight, could see lights on the ground. The clouds were breaking, and we soon saw the airport's runway lights.

I turned the controls back to our chartered VFR pilot.

"You can be captain again. Give us a smooth landing. See if you can stop shaking long enough to 'grease it on,'" I said.

I suggested to the pilot that he spend the night and hope for a VFR flight back to Toronto the next day.

I thought my heart would still be fibrillating after that strange IFR flight the night before, but I got a clear report from the annual physical exam.

When I asked for a lesson with Sam Snead, the traveling golf pro, his assistant said, "You're lucky, Sam isn't here today."

Sam Snead had a well known reputation for conning $100 bets out of business executives while they were eating rich food, drinking wine and otherwise getting healthy at the Greenbriar.

Margy and I played several rounds of golf at that beautiful resort, and we came away more experienced IFR and VFR flyers.

Margy and I had friends in New Canaan who knew the manager of a Rockefeller resort in Virgin Gorda, the easternmost of the British Virgin Islands. This fellow had painted such a glowing picture of the resort that our friends decided to go there for a two-week vacation, and they invited us to join them. The idea appealed to me because I had often thought about taking an island-hopping flight down the thousand-mile trail of the Caribbean islands, so we agreed to go along.

Our friends turned down our invitation to join us at Aero Plantation and fly down with us. They preferred the pains of commercial

flying, seeing nothing, rather than having a lark hopping from island to island and seeing all there was to see.

I got out the charts and maps and laid out a flight plan to Virgin
Gorda. The distance from Charlotte is almost 2,600 miles, beyond
our fuel range and too far for a comfortable one-day flight. We also
had to clear customs before setting off over the Atlantic.

We took off from Aero Plantation with wheels-up at 10 a.m. on
Jan. 12, 1973, and about three hours later we put in at Ft. Lauderdale. There, we rented an inflatable life raft and other emergency
flotation equipment.

Our island-hopping adventure began early the next morning. We
filed a critical flight plan because we had to be cleared to fly through
the U.S. radar-controlled zone.

We quickly climbed out over the Atlantic. At about 2,500 feet, we
picked up the signal from the VOR radio at South Bimini, 70 miles
southeast at 130 degrees, and I clicked on the autopilot to track the
course on our first leg across water. It was a clear morning, and we
observed a patch of clouds ahead, hovering over South Bimini. The
God of the Winds provided us with a patch of clouds directly over
each island for the rest of the trip to reveal not only the islands but
also, usually, the assurance of another landing strip. This confirmed
something I'd heard long before: Clouds form over land.

The weather was terrific. Visibility was unlimited and we could
see for miles ahead, but since we had filed an instrument flight plan,
we were under ATC ground control. They kept us in radar contact
and, from time to time, checked with me to confirm our altitude
and heading.

We quickly passed over Bimini and reset our nav-comm radio to
the Nassau VOR radio, another 115-mile leg on the same southeast-
erly course. Twenty miles out from Nassau, we tuned in 119.5, the
Nassau control tower, and listened in to the controller directing
heavy airline and private traffic in and out of the airport there.

After leaving Nassau, there were plenty of patchy clouds, islands
and landing strips below, but the navigation radio stations dimin-
ished rapidly. Our next VOR was at Grand Turk, 500 miles down
the pike. So for a 100-mile stretch during this leg, we were out of
range of both the Nassau and the Grand Turk stations. ATC told us
that we would be out of radar contact, too.

After nearly three hours, we landed at South Caicos in the Grand
Turk Traffic Control Area. We topped all four tanks with 100-octane

-*Linda Winecoff*

fuel at twice the price we'd paid in Ft. Lauderdale. The line boy didn't seem to care when I added one quart of oil to each engine from my stash in the luggage compartment. To come and go, we filled out long customs forms and paid a big fee. The only bargain there was two delicious lobster rolls and two Cokes for lunch.

We took off from South Caicos, psyched up for the 150-mile, crosswater leap at a heading of 170 degrees south, to a radio station at Puerto Pinta, near Port-au-Prince, Haiti.

During the flight over open water, Margy calmly sat and looked at the ocean and the fuel gauges with very little comment. We flew another 300 miles due east to Saint Thomas, still over water, skirting the northern coast of Puerto Rico. We landed at Virgin Gorda about 5 p.m., more than 1,100 miles and six hours out of Ft. Lauderdale.

We met our friends, who'd arrived at the Rockefeller resort the day before. It was a very relaxing two weeks, with nothing to do but eat great meals, snorkel and nap. I had never snorkeled before, and I found the sport one of the most relaxing I've ever experienced. For hours at a time, we would paddle and kick slowly through the coral passes in water ranging from a few feet to 40 or 50 feet deep, observing thousands of rainbow-colored tropical fish swimming slowly, and darting rapidly, and stationed in small circles to defend their territories.

Another highlight of the trip was a two-hour moonlight sail with the manager of the Virgin Gorda resort, the fellow our friends had known in New Canaan.

Ah, there's romance in the wind and the stars and the moon, sailing along at 15 knots, with the water sloshing over the rails and the halyards slapping against the mast! I hadn't sailed since living near Boston many years before, and this reminded me again of my first flame, Janice. I wondered, as I often do, and I said aloud, "Whatever happened to Janice?"

Margy said, "Who?"

Access to the island was by boat and a small commuter airline headquartered on Saint Thomas, 30 miles to the west. The day before we were scheduled to leave, the airline's maintenance crew went on strike, and service from the island became very erratic.

We required no service at the strip and were able to take off without difficulty, but when we arrived at Saint Thomas and were refueling for the long flight back to South Caicos, a tough-looking union boss emerged from the hangar and told the line boy to stop fueling the Baron. The line boy stopped and put away the hose. We thought we might be in Saint Thomas for the duration of the strike. But when the union toughie went back into the hangar, the line boy sprang into action and rapidly refueled our plane. I paid up fast and we climbed aboard, taxied out and were wheels-up in a jiffy.

We landed again at South Caicos, ate lobster rolls again, refueled and were ready to go.

But just before the customs officer signed the papers and cleared us for departure, he looked at me with pen in hand and said, "I see your next stop is Freeport. And I see you have a vacant back seat in your plane."

"Yes, we're headed that way and hope to touch down there three hours from now," I answered, wondering what he was getting at.

"I have a nephew who has been trying to hitch a ride to Freeport for several months. His uncle is my brother and he works there. He offered to give my boy a place to stay and work if he could find his way to Freeport. Would you mind taking him with you?"

He looked up at me, his potent pen held above the unsigned customs papers. We agreed to take the boy with us, but he wasn't at the airport. The officer said he would have the boy there in five minutes, and he raced off in an ancient, beat-up car that I didn't think would make it past the airport gate, never mind return in five minutes. But the poor heap did return in 10 or 15 minutes with the young boy. We all piled into the Baron, and we were wheels-up out of South Caicos, heading for Freeport, complete with stowaway.

As we climbed to our cruising altitude, Margy and I both noticed a new odor in the plane. Margy accused me of breaking wind.

I felt like saying, "Of course I did. Do you think I smell like this all the time?"

After a few more minutes, we both realized the source of the smell was our young passenger. I wondered if he had ever bathed. We had a stinking, three-hour flight from South Caicos to Freeport.

When we approached the very busy airport there, our passenger's eyes almost popped out of his head as he saw for the first time a metropolitan airport — quite a contrast to the one or two planes, the single windsock and solitary gas pump he was accustomed to at home. But the poor lad was unable to get in touch with his uncle to prove his sponsorship. The customs people tore his small knapsack apart and locked him up in a room down the hall. We never found out what happened to him.

Maybe they sent him back to South Caicos before signing the customs papers for the next pilot who passed through with an empty seat.

By this time, Margy had flown enough to be pretty comfortable, especially flying VFR. Since Kay's accident, I'd grown a little uncomfortable flying in the soup, too, so whenever possible we avoided bad weather. Our timetable had grown more relaxed anyway, so it didn't matter if we had to sit out a day or two waiting for good weather.

The flights to our summer place in Rhode Island had become routine, and the Baron almost knew the three-hour flight from Aero Plantation to Weekapaug by heart. I was a frequent commuter there when I still worked for myself and was managed by money. I have a lot of nostalgia for those flights: taking the last long leg from Atlantic City, over the Atlantic, 60 miles east of New York City, up across Long Island to the last radio station at North Hampton. Then I'd tune in on Providence or New London and let down for 20 miles from 10,000 feet to arrive just off the Weekapaug Inn Beach, only spitting distance above the ocean. I'd advance the throttles to full power and pull back on the stick to send a small, roaring gale down onto the bathers, pull up in a steep turn to 1,000 feet, where I would cut power and glide into the Westerly airport.

Stepping out into a cool, refreshing Rhode Island shore breeze always was a contrast to the 90-degree heat I had left at Aero Plantation three hours before.

When Labor Day ended the summer, we'd take a station wagon overflowing with stuff to the Westerly airport, jam it all into the Baron and head back for Aero Plantation, home for wintertime. It was always as much fun getting back home as it was leaving. We would try to be "wheels up" before 10 a.m. so we would arrive home well before the thunderheads asserted their authority over the skies.

At 10,000 feet, we frequently were on top of a scattered, summertime cloud layer. We would start letting down over Greensboro, N.C., and find a big hole to glide through to avoid being caught up in the turbulent, puffy white stuff. Ten miles out, if the summertime haze wasn't too bad, we could see the lakes, and soon the strip, at Aero Plantation. The strip was in the same direction I had walked before that bulldozer, while holding a compass, so many years before. I would land southeast, uphill, roll out to the end of the strip and taxi back to park at the hangar.

James Richard would be there to meet us. We would unload the ton of luggage, and when we got back to the house with it all, the Rhode Island sweet corn still was as fresh as it was that morning when Mrs. Manfrettie had picked it from the field, and the lobsters were as frisky as if they had never left the salty New England waters.

We invited a few neighbors in and had a last, late summer, Rhode Island feast — before fall came and winter set in.

14

REFLECTIONS ON A CENTURY OF AVIATION

In 1987, I let my flying license lapse by not renewing my annual physical exam, sold my last Baron and my money-management business, and retired to Naples, Florida. But Margy and I have continued to migrate with the Canada geese to Weekapaug, Rhode Island, in May and back to Naples in October.

When we lived, and I worked, in Charlotte, North Carolina, and I owned a Baron, it was an easy three-hour flight from Charlotte to Rhode Island. I could fly Margy there, then easily commute from Charlotte to Rhode Island for a weekend or a month at a time.

After I sold my plane, migrating twice a year from Florida was more difficult. For the first few years, we drove the long 1,700 miles and broke up the trip with visits to family and friends along the way. Then we changed the pattern and would fly commercial, stopping over in Charlotte to visit with old friends.

In the spring of 1996, Margy was anxious to get back to Rhode Island, her favorite of all the places we have lived, so she went ahead to Providence. We shipped the car. I decided to take a slower, stop-and-go journey north.

A few weeks before we left Florida, I'd been studying a fascinating catalogue that listed all the parts and materials one would ever need to build an airplane from a kit. It had pictures and prices for a large variety of kit planes. I was especially taken with the details of the little "E-Racer" two-seater. Power can come from either a modified Buick automobile engine or a standard, four-cylinder Lycoming airplane engine. It cruises at 200 mph and consumes only seven gallons of fuel per hour!

That's almost as fast as the Baron, with one-third less fuel consumption. It has retractable landing gear and a canard wing instead of a tail, so it can't spin. The canard wing is a safety feature that no other commercial or private, single-engine plane has.

I thought I needed a new hobby. Perhaps I could build the E-Racer and have a brand-new, modern, home-built kit plane, maybe ready to solo to celebrate my 80th birthday!

I called Shirl Dickey in Yarnell, Arizona, the E-Racer's designer, and asked if he knew anybody in Florida who was in the later stages of building one. He told me about E.T. Hall, who lived near Blountstown in the Panhandle. Shirl added that he'd worked with Hall for the several years while he was building his plane and knew him as a competent engineer with much airplane experience from a lifelong career in the Air Force.

I called Hall and explained my interest in the E-Racer kit. I asked if I could visit him on my way north, see his plane and talk about his experience building it.

I suspected that I was about to get involved in a tough new hobby when Hall said, "I'd be glad to tell you all about my experience, believe me! Since I started this project, I've wished many times that I'd had the sense to talk to somebody who had built a kit plane.

"Come on up. Land in Blountstown and I'll pick you up there. I keep my Cessna 172 there, and I'll be flying it on Saturday. It's only

The E-Racer kit plane in action   -Courtesy Shirl Dickey

20 miles from where I live."

I chartered a Cessna 310, and the pilot and I flew to Blountstown, 40 miles east of Tallahassee, to visit Hall. The 310 was equipped with a wonderful new navigation instrument called the Global Positioning System, GPS for short. It's about the size of a TV remote control, and it provides a continuous position record with an accuracy of a few meters by receiving information from four satellite transmission signals. With this hand-held device, we found Blountstown's 3,000-foot grass strip on the nose, one mile ahead, in a low overcast and poor visibility.

This was my first experience with a GPS, and I certainly was impressed. I understand this new navigation technology was used to guide missiles down elevator shafts in Iraqi buildings during the Persian Gulf War. I wish they had been available in my flying hey day!

We landed on the rough grass field, and Mr. Hall and his wife were waiting to meet us — the only two lonesome souls standing by a lonesome hanger at the end of the strip. Hall had just finished taking his wife for a spin in his Cessna 172.

As Hall put his wife in the car, he said, "Call me 'Rip,' R-I-P, everybody else does." Then he took me aside and said, "My wife suffers from Alzheimer's Disease."

When my pilot and I climbed in the back seat, Elizabeth Hall turned around, cupped her hand in my direction and said, "I hope you came to buy it," meaning, I assumed, Rip's plane!

"You guys must be ready for lunch," Rip said. "We'll stop a couple of miles down the road where they serve great catfish sandwiches, sweetened ice tea and French fries."

With my curiosity about his E-Racer kit enhanced by my charter pilot's interest, we had a lively discussion during lunch and during the 20-mile ride deep into the desolate pine-tree-farm country, to his modest house with several outbuildings.

There in the garage was his almost-completed E-Racer fuselage sitting on a retractable landing gear. It didn't look anything like ready to fly. It was an inch-and-a-half-thick fiberglass box with an engine hanging on the rear. Most of the cockpit controls were installed, but their cables were still hanging loose outside, waiting for the main wings, winglets and canard wing to be attached. A water-cooled Wankel automobile engine was already mounted, waiting for a propeller.

When Rip sat the canopy on top of the fuselage, it looked more like the pictures I'd seen of the E-Racer. But sitting there without wings, it still looked a little like a go-cart. When I saw how fragile the nose wheel looked, I pushed against the fuselage, and the single wooden strut flexed noticeably without the small wheel moving an inch.

"How about a cross-wind landing?" I asked.

Rip didn't answer.

Two 6x6-inch by 4-foot fiberglass booms extended perpendicular to the rear of the fuselage, just forward of the engine, waiting for the wings to be attached. Foam-rubber seats were installed for two side-by-side passengers in a half-reclining position. Two 8x12-inch openings in the bottom of each side of the instrument-panel wall were cut out for two legs to reach through to the combination rudder and brake pedals. The pedals looked about the size of table-spoons.

"Wanna climb in and see how it sits?" Rip asked.

"Thanks Rip, but I don't see any steps," I replied gingerly.

"We'll get a step ladder!" he chirped.

"I'm afraid I couldn't get in. And if I did, I'm not sure I could get out," I half joked.

I had a vivid memory of the time, way back in 1954, when I first saw a new Ford "T-Bird." It was on display in the lobby of the William Penn Hotel in Pittsburgh. The wife of the friends we were with, who was on the large side, was very interested in the new-model sports car. With some difficulty, she squeezed into the driver's seat to see how it felt. After admiring the car for several minutes, the unlucky lady exercised the handy feature for getting out by pushing the sliding steering column six inches to the right. She tried with all she had but couldn't muster the strength to climb out. It took a careful extraction procedure by the hotel concierge to remove her from that little "T-Bird."

I wanted no part of a similar experience while trying to climb in and out of Rip's E-Racer!

The E-Racer was more of a toy than I'd realized. I hadn't followed the development of the flight-control stick since my early days when I flew the Cub and the Aeronca. The early control sticks were a substantial post that stood between the legs. Then, in the Cessna 152, a horizontal, moving wheel pushed in and out, replacing the stick. The E-Racer had a control stick not much bigger than a large ball-point pen sitting in a console between the seats.

I could see myself, half lying down in that seat, trying to control the flight with a pen-sized stick.

It was just too much when Rip commented, "The throttle can also be incorporated on the control stick, like on the handlebar of a motorcycle."

"Where are the wings?" I asked.

We went to a shed nearby, and there was the canard wing and the two main wings, with ailerons ready to bank the ship, and curt little winglets standing straight up on the ends of each main wing, ready for the rudders to be added to set the course of flight. Two triangular appendages were there, to be installed as gas tanks flared between the fuselage and the wings. Parallel glass pipes would later be installed in the cockpit, and the gas level in the pipes would be a direct measure of the gas level in the tanks. It was an accurate mechanical gas gauge, like the floating cork in the fuel tank of a Piper Cub: Better than the electrical system in a Boeing 747.

After my pilot and me had exhausted our questions, I thanked Rip for his hospitality.

"You met us at the airport, wanted to buy our lunch, drove us 20 miles to your workshop and have spent an hour and a half explaining your three years of work on this kit plane. And now you're ready to return us to the strip. You're very kind and generous with your time," I said.

"That's because I knew how badly you needed someone to square with you about a job whose magnitude you can't imagine," Rip said.

He'd been at it for two years, and it looked as though he had another year, maybe two, to go.

When we got back to the strip, I said goodbye to Rip and thanked him again. When I bade farewell to Rip's wife, Elizabeth, she said again, "I hope you're gonna buy it!"

My pilot flew me on to Gregg field at Jacksonville. This chartered flight from Naples to Jacksonville, with the remote stop-off in Blountstown, reminded me of the old days when I had my own plane and could hop off to anywhere whenever I pleased.

When I sold my plane 10 years ago, I thought I would charter planes and maintain the convenience of private flying, but I've done it only half a dozen times because it's so expensive compared with commercial flying.

That night I called Margy up in Rhode Island.

"How'd you like the kit plane you went to see? And what advice did you get about building one?" Margy asked.

"It was a very interesting toy. I was afraid to climb aboard and sit in it for fear I couldn't get out. I'll talk to the designer and see if we can add a few inches to the length and several inches to the height," I responded, knowing full well that it would involve redesigning the plane.

After I returned to Weekapaug, I found that Margy had told everybody we knew about my experience with Rip, and they were all laughing about my plans to build a new toy. A few years before this, I thought I'd already purchased my last toy, a red golf cart with a simulated Rolls Royce body. A lot of my friends are still laughing about that, too.

Two days after my encounter with Rip Hall, a dawn taxi delivered me to the Jacksonville airport, where I caught a USAir flight to Charlotte. Shortly after we passed over Columbia, South Carolina, cruising at 33,000 feet, I noticed the noise of the jet had decreased. I knew the pilot had throttled back the engines to begin the long descent into Charlotte.

Peering out the right-side window, I saw the Catawba River, and pretty soon I spotted Lancaster. I could see the large Springs Co. textile mills along the highway between Lancaster and Chester. This took me back to 1923, 72 years before, when I saw Col. Elliot Springs, the dashing World War I ace, on his memorable flight under the Buster Boyd Bridge.

I spotted the new Lancaster County airport between Lancaster and the river, and I pondered about the life of Elliot Springs, who had long ago outgrown his flamboyant youth. Following the death of his father, Leroy Springs, he had inherited the mills and became a textile magnate in his own right. On the way from his youth to his business leadership, he was an author and an advertising man of some renown.

His claim to fame in advertising was an ad that showed a tired Indian lying in bed, with an ill-clad maiden sitting beside him. The caption read, "A well-spent Buck on Springs Made Sheets."

Col. Springs kept a plane and a glider at the Lancaster County airport, and his only son, Sunny, learned to fly there. On Mother's Day in 1946, Col. Springs was flying his plane, pulling a glider flown by his son and an instructor. When the tow rope was released, the glider stalled, then crashed, killing both the instructor and the colonel's only son.

I was working in Schenectady, N.Y., at the time, and my mother sent me clippings from the *Lancaster News* that described the tragic event. My mother was a member of the Lancaster County Library Board, along with a Mrs. Rice. Mr. Rice was a director and the chief financial officer of Springs mills and one of the colonel's closest associates. In Mother's letter she described meeting Mrs. Rice a few weeks after the accident. Her description of the devastation of Col. Elliot White Springs was one of the saddest stories I had ever heard about an aviation accident.

Aviation accidents carry a public horror that automobile accidents don't. On my USAir flight over Lancaster that afternoon, I could see 10,000 houses in Lancaster, each with a family. In most of those families during the past 75 years, there almost certainly had been car accidents of similar sadness to the families involved. But the single accident remembered by all Lancaster residents for a long time was the Springs glider tragedy.

I watched the Catawba River from the plane window as we continued our descent into Charlotte. A lot of water has flowed down the Catawba since I was seven years old and my brother John Ed taught me to swim it from shore to shore. I still remember that feel of the mud oozing between my toes as I got my footing back on shore after swimming across and back.

And I remember John Ed's smile as he extended his hand to help me ashore, saying, "Jim you've conquered the river, but we better not tell Mother about it yet. She doesn't even know that we can swim!"

We flew on. Van Wyck sat quietly on the eastern side of the river. I could see light smoke from the kilns at what used to be the Ashe Brick Co., now owned by a foreign conglomerate. On the east side of the Catawba River, stretching five miles north of Van Wyck, I could see the 2,000 acres of land that Uncle Jim had owned and that my dad had farmed for him. This was the very same land my father and my mother thought I would own one day, since they had bowed to Uncle Jim's request and named me James Douglas Nisbet II.

In the summer of 1932, three months after I told Uncle Jim, "I don't want to be a doctor," my dad and I were called to an emergency at his house, half a mile from ours. We arrived in time to see an ambulance waiting, and to see Uncle Jim being carried to it on a stretcher. He had suffered a heart attack the night before, but he was conscious enough to feebly lift his hand in recognition, to say goodbye. Uncle Jim died that night in the Charlotte hospital.

A few days after the funeral, we learned that immediately after my confrontation with Uncle Jim about his plan for me to study medicine at Duke, both my dad and I had been cut out of his will. This was a blow to my dad, but it never bothered me that much. I was a cocky teenager, ready to bounce off to college to make my own way, and my own fortune.

Aunt Beulah survived Uncle Jim by 30 years, and the land was finally equally divided between 11 nieces and nephews, so my dad's share, as a nephew, was 1/11. That was divided among dad's 7 children, who were great nieces and nephews. My share was 1/77 of the assets, 26 acres of land and a few shares of Lucky Strike cigarette stock.

I spent several days in Charlotte, revisiting old haunts and recalling some earlier flying experiences. My USAir flight was only one of almost 500 flights a day now serving Charlotte. USAir now dominates the luxurious Charlotte airport, with 85 percent of the commercial traffic.

I remembered landing at Charlotte on my first commercial flight in December 1940. I was flying on an Eastern Airlines DC3, and traffic then was only four or five planes a day.

When Douglas built the twin-engine DC3, it cruised at 150 mph, fast enough to get the first passengers off of trains and into the air. It really marked the introduction of commercial aviation.

The Ford Tri-Motor came out a few years earlier, but it was too sluggish to gain a foothold. Hanger talk at airports still chides the Ford "Flying Goose" because, they say, "It takes off at 90 mph, has a top speed of 90 mph, cruises at 90 mph and lands at 90 mph."

DC3s still fly. I saw one recently when I was playing golf. They're used in Naples to spray chemicals for mosquito control, but only occasionally, when the environmentalists aren't looking or are sleeping late.

Fifteen years ago, the now defunct Provincetown-Boston Airlines and little Air New England still flew DC3s. I flew in one in 1985 from Naples, and we had an engine failure a few miles outside of Tampa. The Captain didn't hesitate before making a 180-degree turn and returning to Naples on one engine. He knew the DC3 could fly all day on one fan.

On the flight back to Naples, I remember looking out the window at the stilled, feathered propeller on the dead engine. I could see loose rivets popping in and out of holes in the blackened engine cowlings! When we landed at Naples, I climbed out of the DC3 onto the step provided, expecting to transfer to the airline's newer, 12-passenger Cessna, but when the attendant pointed us toward the replacement plane, it was the airline's other DC3! I climbed back up another step outside the door and entered the cabin. The second DC3 got us to Tampa without further mishap, but a little late. It also had rivets popping in and out of holes in the engine cowlings!

Perhaps this is evidence that the FAA really does allow old-timer commuter planes to fly with less rigid maintenance rules than those imposed on bigger carriers. It was a charge leveled at the agency after several commuter-plane crashes in the early 1990s.

Larger planes, of course, have more than three wheels. The Boeing 747 has 18, 16 in the rear and only two in the nose. I've heard the hanger story that when a young Boeing engineer was designing the landing gear for the 747, he asked a long-haul truck driver how many wheels he had.

"I drive an eighteen-wheeler," the trucker replied.

So the young engineer said, "That should be enough for the 747, too."

I guess that 90 percent of the 747's weight is supported on the rear wheels and only 10 percent by the front wheels, just enough up front to give it good traction for steering while it taxis.

Again, hanger talkers call a good three-point landing, whether by a taildragger or not, "greasing it on." Even today, when I depart from a commercial flight and see the captain of the ship standing outside his cockpit bidding passengers, "Goodbye, and have a nice day," he gives me a fellow pilot's understanding with a big grin when I say, "You really greased it on!"

The commercial, half-million-pound Boeing 747 monster with a tricycle landing gear can be "greased on" and it's a sight to see!

My first close-up view of a 747 landing was in 1971, the first year the aircraft was approved for commercial flight. I was sitting in my Baron on the taxiway at the Toronto airport, waiting as number two in line for clearance to take off, when a huge plane appeared on a

The mighty Boeing 747 comes in for a landing.

close final. When it crossed the fence, the threshold of the active runway, traveling 30 or 40 feet off the ground at 170 mph, I could tell it was a 747 because of its unique fuselage.

It's three stories high. The pilot's cabin and a passenger's lounge are on the top deck, above the main passenger cabin. I remember the configuration very well because in 1975 I flew in a TWA 747, 14 hours non-stop, from Hong Kong to Los Angeles.

The picture here, courtesy of Bruce Bowers, a retired TWA 747 pilot, shows this mammoth plane in a landing configuration.

The wings are flat as a pancake when the plane flies at 35,000 feet, at 50 degrees below zero, cutting through the air at 500 mph. But as I watched that landing configuration that day in Toronto, the flaps hung 15 feet straight down below the trailing edge of the wings. The slats, slots, or just call 'em leading-edge devices, protruded four feet below the leading edge of the wings. As the 747 descended to the runway, its 16 rear wheels hung in disarray waiting to be leveled when they smoked onto the pavement 500 feet beyond the threshold of the runway.

Just above the ground, the wings disfigure into a huge, upside-down "U" shape that looks like anything but a lamella airfoil but still supports hundreds of tons.

At this stage, the monstrous ship's attitude appears to be in take-off position, with the nose pointing 10 to 15 degrees up in the air and the two side-by-side nose wheels hanging below the nose 65 feet above the ground.

I imagined the pilot, six stories up. He had to have his wits about him, feeling by the seat of his pants for a spot on the ground, watching his radio altimeter, waiting to stall in the nick of time. When the first of the ship's 16 rear wheels touched down, a domino effect followed as the other wheels cascaded to level positions and smoked onto the ground.

As I sat there on the Toronto taxiway, the 747 rolled on another 1,000 feet before the nose wheels finally, gracefully, descended to the pavement, like a bird dog putting his paw to the ground after holding a point.

Then the spoilers, hinged to the leading edge of the top side of the wing, popped vertically up and added hundreds of square feet of drag to help slow down the huge craft. A blast came from the four engines' 50,000-pound reverse thrusters to counteract the continuing forward movement. This reverse thrust, coupled with the spoilers and wheel brakes, stopped the 450,000 pound bird, but only after inertia carried it a second mile down the runway. There it turned and taxied toward the terminal.

I could no longer see it, but I knew from watching those birds before from the terminal that after the landing gear and all the other mechanical contrivances have done their duty, the pilot commenced to flick more switches and pull more levers. This sucked back in all the "legs, feet and hands" that had hung from the front and back of the wings as the big ship rolled on those monstrous 18 wheels. A few minutes before, the shafts, landing lights, wires and hydraulic hoses connected to the array of disk brakes had all been behind sealed doors in the bottom of the fuselage, away from the tremendous drag they would impose if exposed to normal flight.

I drove 10 miles from my hotel in Charlotte to Aero Plantation, the 500-acre residential real-estate development I had founded 33 years before. As a frustrated architect, I was always curious to see what the new houses looked like.

The landing strip at Aero Plantation attracted many of the early homeowners. Today, only seven of the 85 owners have planes. It's obvious that features other than the landing strip, like large wooded lots, 65 acres of lakes, and private roads bordered by beautiful trees, and a quiet countryside, have been more important reasons for Aero's growth into a posh residential community that happens to have a landing strip.

I hadn't been to the new Monroe airport for several years, so I drove over there to see what had happened lately. It had grown a great deal since the time I bought 400 acres and sold 100 through the middle of it to the city for the airport, leaving the surrounding 300 acres for an industrial park.

Surely I'd sold my interest in it too soon! As an investor, I always seem to violate one of the cardinal principles of the trade — patience.

As I stood on the knoll above the reception building I had given to the city in memory of Kay, in 1970, I remembered the late Bob Morrison, a close friend, whom I'd flown with many times. He was Dickerson's pilot for his entire career. He retired when the Dickerson Co. bought a new Beech King Air. Bob couldn't stand to part com-

An Army version of the Twin Beech.

pany with the Twin Beech he'd flown for so many years.

During his flying career, Bob Morrison flew three successive models of this taildragging Twin Beech out of the old Monroe airport. And he did it with only an ADF tuned to the Monroe radio station to navigate his passengers and himself home on cold, rainy nights. He landed on that 2,500-foot grass strip for 30 years without an accident, and, he told me, he twice came in on one engine.

Before executive jets arrived, the Twin Beech probably was the most popular executive plane. A few years after World War II, it and similar internal-combustion engine planes were replaced by turboprops, like the King Air. Then the Learjet captured the jet market.

The Gulfstream V

Today, there are thousands of executive aircraft, with jet planes of many varieties. In addition to the Learjet, which my old friend Hank Rowan flies, there's the Cessna Citation, the Hawker Sidney, a Beechcraft jet, the DH125, and the real top of the line, the Gulfstream V pictured above —the brand Jack Nicklaus flies and advertises.

Standing on that knoll, I suddenly spotted a Cessna Citation, parked on the ramp for refueling. By Jove, it was the jet bought by the Teledyne executive who had replaced me when I resigned in 1970! I've never had a ride in it.

Executive aircraft, like commercial planes, have new contraptions on the front, back and top of the wings, in addition to flaps, foils, slots, slats and spoilers. The big commercial, military and executive jets can fly faster, land slower with heavier loads and consume less fuel with these newer, efficient wings.

For another touch of efficiency, winglets have been added to the ends of wings to subdue the continuous little cyclones that spring up out there and add drag and reduce lift. They're little extensions of the wing that stick up a few feet out there on the end. In my opinion, they also add beauty, as illustrated by this picture of the Gulfstream V.

I drove over to the Rock Hill, S.C., airport and was surprised to find that the young lady, Senna, who had been Jim Duncan's co-pilot on the Cheyenne turboprop that Tom Roboz so frequently chartered, was now manager of the airport. She told me that Lindsay Hess, the former manager, recently had completed a five-year contract stunt flying for the Carowinds theme park near Charlotte.

Senna's husband was his partner. She said Lindsay was managing the Salisbury airport north of Charlotte.

I wondered what had happened to the glider school at the airport in Chester, S.C., where Kay and I had gone almost 30 years before to get checked out and to solo in a glider after we had missed our flight to Europe in the Baron. I called there, and learned that the glider school had moved to a new airport in Lancaster County, near Kershaw. I had to see it!

I was impressed with the glider school's new name, *Bermuda High Soaring*. It's now operated by Jayne and Frank Reid. Jayne Reid set a 30,000-foot glider altitude record in 1989. I saw the huge hanger where their two school gliders and half a dozen private ones are housed.

Two high-powered, low-speed, dust-cropping Piper Pawnees were parked outside. It's the plane preferred for towing gliders aloft.

I noticed that the gliders, I believe without exception, were made not of aluminum or wood, but of composite materials such as fiberglass and graphite, the same high-tech materials used in fishing rods, $500 golf-club shafts and kit planes of all varieties, including the world-circling Voyager and the E-Racer.

When Margy and I settled back in Rhode Island for the summer in 1996, I realized the events of the past few weeks had disturbed my peace of mind. Being totally absorbed with writing this book over the previous winter, I became so wrapped up in it that I must have reached my second childhood, an old man wanting to fly again.

To further pursue that idea of building a kit plane and getting back into the air, I went to the Experimental Aircraft Association (EAA) show in Oshkosh, Wisconsin. This is the Mecca for home kit builders, restorers, ultralights, war birds, aircraft-parts flea markets, continuous technical sessions on all aspects of aviation, and a daily, two-hour acrobatic show that always leaves you breathless.

It's a convention for all ages: pilots and planes ranging from World War II types to young families pulling their kids in wagons for miles around the tarmac; and planes ranging from old Stearman mail planes to the Concorde and the B1 Bomber.

Both the EAA Oshkosh show and the Lakeland, Fla., "Fun in the Sun" show have been produced for the past quarter century with

Burt Rutan as the guru and Paul H. and Tom Poberezny as the founders/promoters.

And pilots! It looked as though 3,000 had flown in and pitched tents by their planes. *Flying* magazine reported that 800,000 people attended the 1996 show and that 10,000 airplanes landed there during the week!

On the third day, as I walked out to search for my car in the huge parking lot, people were saying Rutan had flown out that morning in his latest creation, an unusual twin-engine that he had named "Boomerang." It didn't have a canard wing, his trademark in airplane design, but it did have the strangest second, smaller engine mounted on a smaller left wing boom.

And nobody seemed to know why. Rutan compared the performance of this five-passenger, pressurized personal plane with the popular Beechcraft Baron. The Boomerang cruises at 311 mph, 30 percent faster than the six-place Baron, has almost twice the range, consumes 50 percent less fuel and flies with one 200- and one 210-hp engine versus two 350-hp engines in the pressurized Baron.

In a final touch, the fifth seat can be used as a bed. Now I understood.

What's happened to our three most popular general aviation companies, Beechcraft, Piper and Cessna? I don't believe they've introduced a new light twin in 25 years. It's ironic when we remember that Rutan designed the Starship for Beechcraft and was a VP there for a while.

The "Velocity," one of Burt Rutan's revolutionary aircraft designs

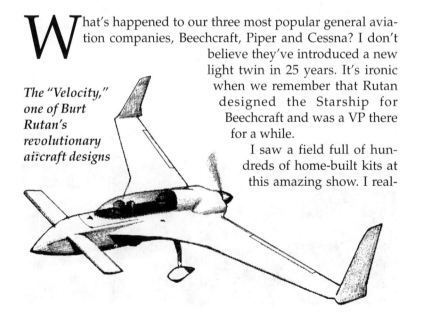

I saw a field full of hundreds of home-built kits at this amazing show. I real-

146

ized that Shirley's E-Racer wasn't the only alternative for a home-built plane, and a new avenue for me to fly again opened before my eyes. Two other designs struck my fancy. One was a conventional design, without Rutan's canard wing, but built with the modern-day composites of fiberglass and graphite. It was called the Lancair, a sleek, four-place, pressurized fiberglass and graphite composite that cruises at 300 mph with a 500-hp Nasion automobile engine.

Also of interest to me was another modification of the Rutan designs that looked much like Shirley's E-Racer. Called the "Velocity," it's a four-place, canard-wing, 200-hp, 200-mph pusher. It's significantly different from the E-Racer, with four comfortable bucket seats in a larger cabin and doors for entry and exit rather than a canopy entrance.

Rip hadn't shown me how the Long-EZ, the E-Racer and many other copycat Rutan kits are parked — by lowering the front-wheel landing gear until the nose sits on the ground. It was funny to see dozens of Long-EZs and their sisters, brothers and cousins — all copycats — kneeling on their noses at Oshkosh. With the nose lowered, they look like a camel kneeling, ready to be mounted by an Arab sheik. It's practical Rutan: They may look ridiculous, but they certainly are easier to get into and out of with a lowered nose!

The Author checks out a Long-EZ at the Oshkosh show.
-Collection of the Author

Of course, all planes in the '20s and '30s sat on their tails, with two high front wheels and a low tail wheel or a dragging spring. They were appropriately called "taildraggers." Lindbergh's "Spirit of St. Louis," the barnstormer's Stearman, the mail carrier's Waco and the commercial DC3 all were taildraggers, and they all were at Oshkosh.

I recalled that, even as late as World War II, the taildragger was king. The B17 bomber, of the sort my friend Pete Rosin flew during the war, sat with the "warbirds" at Oshkosh. The B17 was one of the first warplanes equipped with the General Electric turbo-supercharger that enabled it to fly at 20,000 feet or higher and still maintain full power. It stunted with the best stunt planes at Oshkosh.

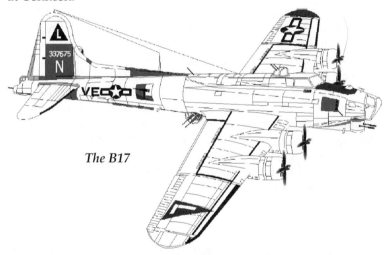

The B17

On the ground, the B17 is stark and ugly. But it was a graceful bird flying at 20,000 feet while returning from a bombing mission over Europe. Letting down over the English Channel, headed for home, it must have been quite a sight, even if it was shot up a little, and possibly limping, because one of the supercharger blades had failed.

I paid $2 to go through a B17 Bomber. I climbed up an eight-rung ladder and squeezed through a hatch about the size of a manhole cover. I climbed on hands and knees for several feet before I could stand behind the pilot's cockpit and the forward machine gun turrets, above the huge, open bomb bay. I darn near got stuck while coaxing my substantial middle through the narrow passage across the bomb bay. Forward, in the tail, on each side and in the top and bottom, there were more machine-gun turrets.

As I climbed through the B17, I could imagine the raw terror and claustrophobia of the young GI gunners as they sat down and buckled themselves in, prepared to man the machine-gun stations as my friend, Capt. Pete Rosin, shouted through the intercom, "Ready for take-off."

I could also feel their terror in flight, and their sense of exhausted relief, when, 10 hours later, completely spent, they returned to England, and Capt. Rosin shouted, "Cleared to land."

I noticed that the B25 sitting beside the B17 had a tricycle landing gear. It was designed in 1939 by Consolidated Aircraft, now General Dynamics, and was no doubt one of the very first Army bombers to have a tricycle landing gear.

I inspected the GE supercharger that hung under each of the four 1,200-hp Pratt and Whitney radial engines that powered these birds. I wondered if I might have seen those same superchargers when I was the chief metallurgist in the Indiana GE plant where they were manufactured during World War II. I noticed, too, that they were late-model superchargers. I could tell because each had a late-war retrofit below the turbine wheel. This was a deflector designed to suck in the cold, high-altitude air and blow it against the hot turbine wheel to lower its temperature and prolong its life. It also reduced the chance that they might blow up in bad places, like on a bombing run over Berlin.

In marked contrast to the B17, the most modern Air Force ship was sitting on the ground at Oshkosh, taking up a lot of room with its 150-foot wingspread: the B2 Stealth Bomber.

The Concorde, the English/French plane that flies faster than sound, at Mach 2, had been at Oshkosh the year before. The Concorde is a novelty because it was built by a consortium of British and French companies, and everybody knows such a feat was an impossible undertaking, or nearly so.

On my way back to Florida in October 1996, I visited Velocity, the company in Sebastian, Fla., that designed the Velocity plane. I had a ride in their demonstrator, and the pilot let me fly it. I felt like a kid again, flying a Piper Cub. It was amaz-

*The B2
"Stealth"
Bomber*

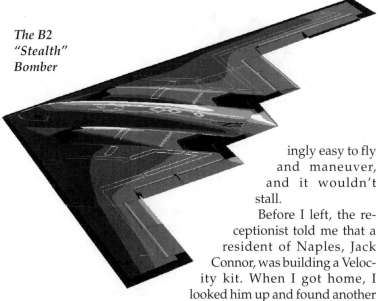

ingly easy to fly
and maneuver,
and it wouldn't
stall.

Before I left, the re-
ceptionist told me that a
resident of Naples, Jack
Connor, was building a Velocity kit. When I got home, I
looked him up and found another
'Rip Hall' in his garage, two years into his home-built Velocity kit
project. Jack lives only ten blocks from where I live in Naples. I'll
follow the progress of that one until it takes off, and maybe I can
have a turn at the controls of that one too.

T he Wright brothers introduced powered aviation to this century with their first flight. It would appear that the Rutan
brothers are closing the century as the greatest innovators of
modern aircraft design. Who will top brother Dick Rutan, who with
Jeanne Yeager, in 1989, flew the Burt Rutan-designed Voyager non-
stop around the world without refueling?

I would submit the proposition that neither the Wright brothers,
nor Lindbergh nor Sir Frank Whittle nor the Voyager trio could have
accomplished their missions and great expeditions if they *had* been
government sponsored with unlimited funds. Nor could these feats
ever have been accomplished by a committee of engineers in a cor-
poration.

Most of history's greatest events speak for the uncanny ability of
individuals to do remarkable things when their spirits are set free
and there is a fire within them.

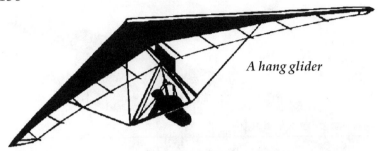

A hang glider

My 80th birthday came and went, and I didn't get started on building either the E-Racer or the Velocity kit. But I haven't given up on the idea.

In the meantime, I want to climb to the top of Grandfather Mountain in North Carolina, get harnessed up in a hang glider, race to the edge of the cliff and jump off — and solo silently down to the valley below.

I like to think that my own genes contain a few helixes that twist and turn to avoid, rather than conform to, the status quo. That's why flying has been a highlight of my life and why, as I glide on into my 80s, I haven't given up on the idea of getting back into the air!

EPILOGUE

How things turned out

The Kit Plane: After I visited Rip Hall and Jack Conner, who were building two composite constructed kit planes, I drifted back down to earth and admitted to myself that I couldn't possibly find 2,000 spare hours in the 80th year of my life to build a kit plane.

Then I had a bright idea—to have my cake and eat it too. I would buy the kit and give it to the Clemson Flying Club. Club members should be able to get lab credits for building it and they could eventually own it. This would also absolve my shame of 60 years for not having been a very "Giving, Rah, Rah" alumnus. I would kill that bird with the same stone.

I introduced myself by telephone to Dr. Richard Figliola, the current head of the Mechanical Engineering Department at Clemson University..He turned out to be an enthusiastic member of a thriving, 20-man Clemson Flying Club, which did in fact own a tiny fleet, one Cessna 150 for training and one Cessna 172 for flying home.

As I presented my plan and as the conversation progressed, I sensed that the good professor wasn't buying the idea. He said that he shared my enthusiasm for the project, but that I didn't understand the attention span of today's students: It didn't extend to a project of the magnitude I was describing, a semester or two of work for several students. He told me that Clemson and the Clemson Flying Club were not in the same world that I remembered.

I knew my cause was lost when he finally added, "I can see myself having to finish the project alone, but I'll post your idea on the bulletin board and let you know if anybody signs up."

Apparently, nobody did.

Dr. Figliola never called back. I've talked to a number of friends about this disappointing experience with Clemson. It was only a small military college when I was there, and we spent hours on end in lab work. I thought the engineering students in the Flying Club would relish the idea of building their own plane as the club had done in 1930. But then there were no girls at Clemson to frighten, distract and harass the cadets.

ALLVAC: In the late summer of 1996, the manager of human resources at the company I had founded, Allvac Corp. (now an Allegheny Teledyne company) in Monroe, North Carolina, called and said they were planning a celebration for the company's 40th birthday. She asked if I could stop by on Oct. 20 and be in a movie being produced for the occasion. She also invited me to attend the main event on Feb. 8, 1997, I accepted with the following note:

"Mid October is the time of year that we migrate from Rhode Island back to Florida. It is not exactly on the way, but Margy just took off for two weeks in Portugal. Next week I will be headed south by car to Charlotte. I will be in Charlotte three days planting 115 Leyland cypress trees at Aero Plantation and can come by Monroe on Friday morning for the movie interview.

"Then I will be off on a Frequent Flyers round trip to California for a long weekend with my children. I will pick up my car back in Charlotte and drive to Naples with a two-night rest stop with my daughter Holly in Ponte Vedra, Fla.

"Certainly, I don't want to miss being in the movie or the 40th anniversary celebration of the founding of Allvac. I will certainly be there, but tell John Andrews it would help a weary traveler if he would send his jet down from Monroe to Naples to pick me up."

The Allvac jet, a Cessna Citation, met me at the Naples airport at 9 a.m. on Feb. 8, 1997, with a pilot and a co-pilot no less. I climbed aboard and we taxied out. The captain took off, pointed the nose of the sleek ship 25 degrees skyward and headed north. I got goose pimples listening to the shrill noise of the hot gases coursing over Allvac's red-hot, super-alloy blades and veins and then expanding through the powerful jet engines to thrust me back in time at 500 miles per hour toward what had been *my company.*

Allvac's Cessna Citation,
and Allvac President John Andrews

The Author

James D. Nisbet grew up in Lancaster County, South Carolina, and attended Clemson College during the Great Depression. He graduated in 1937 with a B.S. in engineering and a lifelong love of the pleasures and mechanics of flying. While working for General Electric during World War II, he developed a process for manufacturing materials for gas turbines. In 1957, he founded the Allvac Metals Co. in Monroe, North Carolina, and later served as Group V.P. at Teledyne Corp. Since 1970, he has been a venture capitalist, money manager, stock-market researcher and the author of five books.

Today, Jim and his wife, Margy, divide their year between their summer home in Weekapaug, Rhode Island, and their winter abode in Naples, Florida.

Index